Carpentry and Joinery

and

LEVEL 2

Peter Brett

Published in 2011 by:
Nelson Thornes Ltd
Delta Place
27 Bath Road
CHELTENHAM
GL53 7TH
United Kingdom

11 12 13 14 15 / 10 9 8 7 6 5 4 3 2 1

A catalogue record for this book is available from the British Library

ISBN 978 1 4085 0881 7

Cover photographs by Erkki Makkonen/iStockphoto and Zack Blanton/iStockphoto
Illustrations by Peters & Zabransky (UK) Ltd and Pantek Arts Ltd
Page make-up by Pantek Arts Ltd, Maidstone

Printed and bound in Spain by GraphyCems

Acknowledgements

Alamy p34b (Paula Solloway), p67b (David J. Green – construction themes), p75b (Arthur Gebuys – gebuys.com) p75c (Paul Williams); **Anant** p112c; **Construction photography** p40b (David Potter), p40c (Jean-Francois Cardella); **Fotolia** p29 (Sebastian Duda); **Ikea** p62a, p62b; **Instant art** p25, p26; **iStockphoto** p1, p13a, p13b p21a, p21b, p21c, p21d, p34a, p37, p40a, p41a, p42, p45, p55, p66, p74, p83, p91, p103, p111; **Rentokil Property Care** p75a (www.rentokil.co.uk/propertycare); **Screwfix/ McCann Erickson PR** p41b p67a, p67c; **Toolbank Marketing Services** p112b; **1066 Tools** p112a.

Contents

Introduction

Welcome to the Carpentry and Joinery Course Companion Level 2. It is literally a companion to support you throughout your course and record your progress!

This workbook-style book is designed to be used alongside **any** student book you are using. It is packed full of activities for you to complete in order to check your knowledge and reinforce the essential skills you need for this qualification.

Features of the Course Companion are:

Unit opener – a brief introduction to each unit

Key knowledge – the underpinning knowledge you must know is summarised at the beginning of each unit

Activities – a wide variety of learning activities are provided to complete in your Companion. Each activity is linked to one of the Personal, Learning and Thinking Skills to help you practise these fundamental skills:

– Reflective Learner   – Self Manager

– Creative Thinker   – Independent Enquirer

– Teamworker   – Effective Participator

You will also notice additional icons that appear on different activities. These link to the following core skills and also to rights and responsibilities in the workplace:

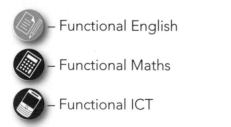

– Functional English

– Functional Maths

– Functional ICT

– Employment, Rights and Responsibilities

Key terms – during your course you will come across new words or terms that you may not have heard before, so definitions for these have been provided

Your questions answered – your expert author, Peter Brett, answers some burning questions you may have as you work through the units

Quick quiz – At the end of each unit you will find a multiple-choice quiz. Answering these will check that you have fully understood what you have learned.

Good luck!

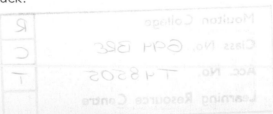

UNIT 1001

Safe working practices in construction

Health and safety forms an essential part of your daily working life. Ensuring that a site is as safe as it possibly can be is a shared responsibility between employers and the workforce.

Employers have a duty to create safe working conditions and provide the workforce with training that explains safety rules, procedures and regulations.

You, as part of the workforce, have a major contribution to make to site safety. You can do so by responding to safety instructions, complying with safety rules and developing the skills to identify potential safety hazards and reduce risks.

While at work you must comply with a wide range of legislation, regulations and supporting approved codes of practice (ACoP). Health and safety legislation is there to protect all persons at their place of work and other people from the risks occurring through work activities.

Key knowledge:
➤ health and safety regulations, roles and responsibilities
➤ accident and emergency procedures and how to report them
➤ hazards on construction sites
➤ health and hygiene in a construction environment
➤ how to handle materials and equipment safely
➤ basic working platforms
➤ how to work with electricity in a construction environment
➤ how to use personal protective equipment (PPE) correctly
➤ fire and emergency procedures
➤ safety signs and notices.

Health and safety regulations

Abbreviations and legislation

Health and safety **legislation**, people and organisations are often referred to by abbreviations or initials. You should be able to recognise these and know what they mean.

Your questions answered...

What can happen to me or my employer if health and safety legislation or approved codes of practice are not followed?

Failure to comply with the requirements of a piece of legislation or a set of **regulations** is a criminal offence that could result in prosecution. Failure to comply with an **ACoP** is not in itself an offence but, if a contravention of the associated regulations is alleged, failure to follow the ACoP will be accepted as evidence in a court of law.

ACTIVITY

Match each abbreviation concerned with health and safety legislation with its appropriate description:

	The main legislation that covers health and safety at work.
PPER	
	The body responsible for the enforcement of health and safety in the UK.
COSHH	
	Places a **duty** on employers, the self-employed and persons in control of premises to report to the HSE some accidents and incidents at work.
HASAWA	
	Requires employers to control exposure to hazardous substances in the workplace to prevent ill-health and protect both employees and others who may be exposed.
RIDDOR	
	Requires all duty holders including the client, designers, building contractors, sub-contractors, site workers and others to play their part in improving onsite health and safety.
MHO	
	Requires employers and the self-employed to avoid the need to undertake manual handling operations that might create a **risk** of injury.
HSE	
	Requires employers to provide employees with any necessary personal equipment that is needed in order to carry out work safely.
CDM	

Duties under health and safety legislation

Duties in legislation can be either 'absolute' or have a qualifying term added, namely 'reasonably practicable'.

ACTIVITY

In a group, discuss whether each of the duties below applies to a) employers, b) employees or c) designers, manufacturers and suppliers

- Report **hazards**, accidents and near misses. ____
- Take reasonable care at all times and ensure that their actions or omissions do not put at risk themselves, their workmates or any other person. ____
- Provide and maintain safe machinery, equipment and methods of work. ____
- Ensure that equipment, machinery or material is designed, manufactured and tested so that when it is used correctly no hazard to health and safety is created. ____
- Ensure safe access to and from the workplace. ____
- Ensure the safe handling, transport and storage of all machinery, equipment and materials. ____
- Never misuse or interfere with anything provided for health and safety. ____
- Carry out research so that any risk to health and safety is eliminated or minimised as far as possible. ____

key terms

Absolute: means that the requirement must be met regardless of cost or other implications.

Reasonably practicable: means that you are required to consider the risks involved in undertaking a particular work activity. However, if the risks are minimal and the cost or technical difficulties of taking certain actions to eliminate the risks are high, it might not be reasonably practicable to implement those actions.

Hazard: something with the potential to cause harm.

Harm: can vary in its severity, some hazards can cause death, others illness or disability or maybe only cuts or bruises.

Health and safety facts

ACTIVITY

Choose from the following terms to complete the facts about health and safety:

Induction   Risk assessment   Toolbox   Improvement   HSE   Prohibition   Safety officer

- _____ is the process of identifying hazards, assessing likelihood of **harm** and deciding on adequate control measures.
- An _____ notice issued by an _____ inspector requires employers to put right minor safety hazards within a specified period of time and a _____ notice requires work to stop immediately.
- All new workers to a site must undertake a site safety _____ before starting work.
- Deaths, major injuries and dangerous occurrences must be reported to the _____ without delay.
- _____ talk is the name given to the short talks often on safety topics, given by the site manager or _____.

ACTIVITY

List THREE of the HSE's main powers:

1.

2.

3.

ACTIVITY

In a group, discuss the purpose of toolbox talks and make a list of topics that could be discussed.

Accident and emergency procedures and how to report them

It is important that all accidents, incidents, emergencies and near misses in the workplace are reported, not only to comply with health and safety legislation but also to help prevent recurrences.

Construction is the UK's biggest industry and also one of the most dangerous. The HSE publish data based on the information collected under RIDDOR.

ACTIVITY

This pie chart shows the percentage distribution by severity of reportable accidents in the construction industry.

Undertake research in the library and on the web regarding the main causes of accidents for each of the three categories. Then, using a computer, record your findings in graphical form.

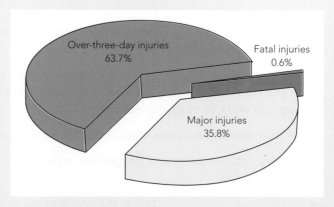

Over-three-day injuries
63.7%

Fatal injuries
0.6%

Major injuries
35.8%

 ACTIVITY

Choose from the following words to fill in the blanks.

Hospital	Diseases	Deaths	Dangerous	Three	Amputations	Infections

Public	Work	Taken	Misses	Injury	Major	Accident

Under RIDDOR, employers, self-employed people and others in control of work premises have a legal duty to inform the HSE of the following events (reportable incidents):

■ _____ arising out of or in connection with work.

■ _____ injuries, which include most fractures, _____ , loss of sight, loss of consciousness, acute illness requiring medical treatment or any other injury involving a stay in _____ .

■ Over-_____ -day injuries where a person is away from _____ or unable to perform their normal work role for more than three consecutive days.

■ Injuries to members of the _____ or people not at work where they are _____ away from the scene of an _____ to hospital.

■ Work-related _____ , which include poisonings, skin diseases, lung diseases, _____ , musculoskeletal disorders and vibration syndrome.

■ _____ occurrences, which include the collapse of a crane, hoist, scaffolding or building, an explosion or fire, or the escape of any substance that is liable to cause a health hazard or major injury to any person.

■ Certain near _____ , where something happens that does not result in an _____ but it could have done, may be classified as dangerous occurrences.

Your questions answered...

Can I go straight home in the event of an emergency rather than reporting to the assembly point?

No, you must follow the evacuation procedures, which are there for everyone's safety. If you don't report to your designated assembly point, other people may be placed at risk trying to find you.

Completing an accident record

Accident records are normally completed by the injured person. If this is not possible, then a witness or someone representing the injured person should complete it.

ACTIVITY

Read the following information:

Andy James is a Site Carpenter who works for BBS Construction and lives at 26 Fields Farm Lane, Long Eaton, Nottingham, NG10 2FF. He is currently working on the Station Road housing estate in Nottingham. At 4.30 p.m. on 18 August 2011, Andy tripped whilst carrying lengths of timber across uneven ground. Andy's reaction was to put out his right hand to break his fall. In doing so he released his grip on the timber, a length of which gave him a glancing blow on the forehead. As a result of this incident an ambulance was called to take Andy to the local hospital for an examination and X-rays. These tests confirmed that Andy had fractured his wrist and would need to wear a plaster cast for four to six weeks. The doctor stated that the blow to Andy's head appeared to have caused severe bruising. Andy was advised to go to his doctor if he suffered any headaches in future.

As a witness to Andy's accident, use this information to complete an accident record.

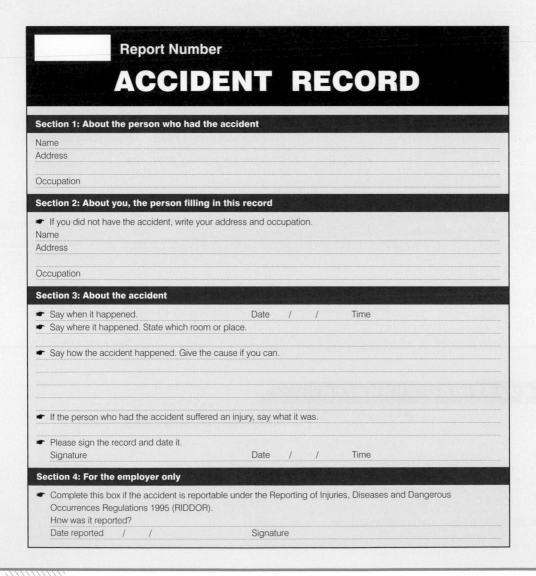

Accident and emergency procedures

ACTIVITY

In a small group discuss why it is important to make a record of an accident and why 'near misses' should be reported.

ACTIVITY

State THREE actions that should be taken by the first person to arrive on the scene of an accident:

1.

2.

3.

Your questions answered...

Why can't my employer keep tablets and medication in the first-aid box?

HSE guidance states that the giving of tablets and medication does not form part of first-aid treatment; therefore they should not be kept in a first-aid kit.

This is because without knowing a person's medical history the use of tablets and other medication can do more harm than good. In addition, if someone did have an allergic reaction as a result of a first-aider administering medication, the first-aider could be sued.

Hazards on construction sites

Carrying out a risk assessment

A risk assessment is a careful examination of the workplace to identify hazards and put measures in place to control the risk of an accident occurring.

ACTIVITY

Consider the five steps to risk assessment:

■ **Step 1.** Look for the hazards.

■ **Step 2.** Decide who might be at risk and how.

■ **Step 3.** Evaluate the risks and decide on the action to be taken.

■ **Step 4.** Record the findings.

■ **Step 5.** Review the findings.

Look around your place of work or your college practical area and identify a hazard. Complete this risk assessment form.

BBS Construction Services

RISK ASSESSMENT

Activity covered by assessment: _____

Location of activity: _____

Persons involved: _____

Dates of assessment: _____

Tick appropriate box ✓

	YES	NO
• Does the activity involve a potential risk?	☐	☐
• If YES can the activity be avoided?	☐	☐

	LOW	MEDIUM	HIGH
• If NO what is the level of risk?	☐	☐	☐

• What remedial action can be taken to control or protect against the risk?

1 _____

2 _____

3 _____

4 _____

5 _____

MANAGEMENT SUMMARY:

Priority for action: LOW ☐ MEDIUM ☐ HIGH ☐

Action to be taken: _____

Date action to be taken by: _____

Date for reassessment: _____

Assessor's name and signature: _____

ASSESS THE RISK - PUT IN CONTROLS - CHECK THEY WORK

Method statements

A method statement is a key safety document, which takes the information about potential risks from a risk assessment and combines them with a job specification.

ACTIVITY

Read this employer's safety method statement concerning the use of MDF panel products. In your own words, describe the risks involved and the correct work procedures to be followed.

BBS: Shopfitting Services
33 Stafford Thorne Street
Nottingham NG22 3RD
Tel. 0115 94000

SAFETY METHOD STATEMENT

Process: **The remanufacture of MDF panel products.** During this process a fine airborne dust is produced. This may cause skin, eye, nose and throat irritation. There is also a risk of explosion. The company has controls in place to minimise any risk. However, for your own safety and the protection of others, you must play your part by observing the following requirements.

General Requirements: At all times, observe the following safety method statements and the training you have received from the company.
- Manual Handling
- Use of Woodworking Machines
- Use of Powered Hand Tools
- General Housekeeping

Specific Requirements:
- When handling MDF, always wear gloves or barrier cream as appropriate. Barrier cream should be replenished after washing.
- When sawing, drilling, routing or sanding MDF, always use the dust extraction equipment and wear dust masks and eye protection.
- Always brush down and wash thoroughly to remove all dust, before eating, drinking, smoking, going to the toilet and finally at the end of the shift.
- Do not smoke outside the designated areas.
- If you suffer from skin irritation or other personal discomfort, seek first-aid treatment or consult the nurse.

IF IN DOUBT ASK

Hazards on construction sites

ACTIVITY

List THREE hazards that are associated with chemical spills in the workplace:

1.

2.

3.

ACTIVITY

Explain THREE safety points concerning the storage of flammable liquids and gases:

1.

2.

3.

ACTIVITY

You are working on a construction site and have been asked to maintain good housekeeping in the workplace. Consider what is meant by this. Using a computer, make a list of what this requires and also any action that should be taken if a hazard is identified in the workplace.

Health and hygiene in a construction environment

Provision of welfare facilities

Welfare facilities include toilets, changing rooms, somewhere to wash, eat and rest and the provision of drinking water. Employers must provide these facilities to ensure health and safety in the workplace.

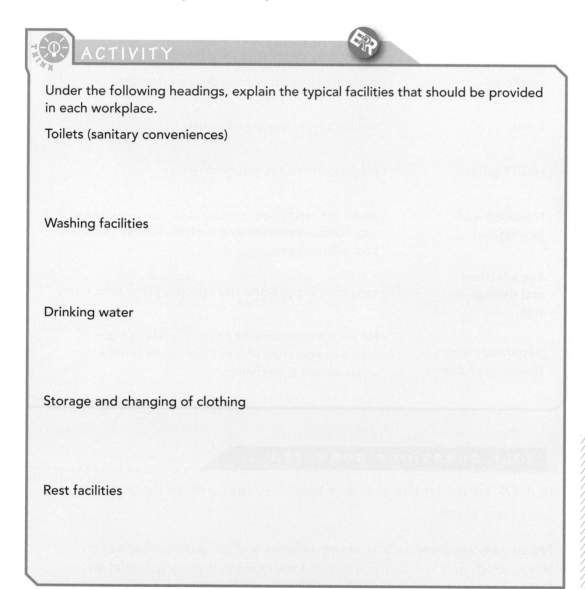

ACTIVITY

Under the following headings, explain the typical facilities that should be provided in each workplace.

Toilets (sanitary conveniences)

Washing facilities

Drinking water

Storage and changing of clothing

Rest facilities

Your questions answered...

Why have I been told at my site induction not to use mobile phones, radios and music players during working hours?

Their use can cause a loss of concentration, as well as interfere with general communications and make emergency warnings, etc. harder to hear.

Health problems associated with construction

The use of chemicals and other hazardous substances are a major risk to people's health on construction sites and other workplaces.

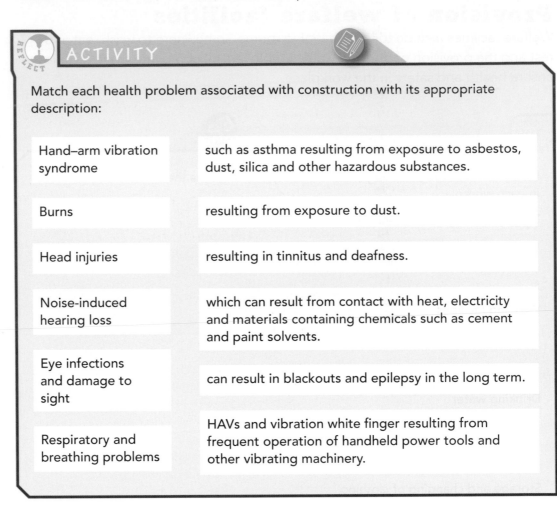

ACTIVITY

Match each health problem associated with construction with its appropriate description:

Hand–arm vibration syndrome	such as asthma resulting from exposure to asbestos, dust, silica and other hazardous substances.
Burns	resulting from exposure to dust.
Head injuries	resulting in tinnitus and deafness.
Noise-induced hearing loss	which can result from contact with heat, electricity and materials containing chemicals such as cement and paint solvents.
Eye infections and damage to sight	can result in blackouts and epilepsy in the long term.
Respiratory and breathing problems	HAVs and vibration white finger resulting from frequent operation of handheld power tools and other vibrating machinery.

Your questions answered...

Is it OK to go to the pub and have just one pint of beer during a lunchtime break?

No, as just one drink leads to slower reflexes and reduced concentration levels, which puts not only you but also everyone in the workplace at an increased risk of danger. In addition, it is almost certainly against your employer's safety policy, which you would have been advised of during your induction, and doing this could result in your dismissal.

ACTIVITY

Produce a list of FOUR precautionary control measures that may be taken to prevent or reduce exposure to hazardous substances:

1.

2.

3.

4.

Handle materials and equipment safely

Mechanical and manual handling aids

Manual handling should only be undertaken as the last resort after considering all other mechanical means and manual aids available.

ACTIVITY

Look at the photographs in the margin, which show some mechanical and manual handling aids. Name each item and describe a situation where each would be suitable to use:

A

B

How much can I safely lift and when should I seek help?

Although the maximum load that one person should move is 25 kg, it is dependent on your stature and competence. Two or more persons are required to move heavier, larger or awkward shaped items to reduce the risk of injury.

Mechanical versus manual handling

ACTIVITY

Either in a small group or on your own, consider the following real-life problem or scenario:

Kevin and John work as a pair and have been employed by a sub-contract carpentry firm for the last six months working on a large housing project. When they arrived for work one morning, there was a lorry containing long floor **joists** at the site entrance. They decided to offload the joists by hand as the plant driver had not yet arrived.

While collecting one of the timber joists from the vehicle's driver, John lost his footing on the uneven ground. He twisted quickly in an attempt to maintain his balance, but ended up in a heap on the ground, with the joist giving him a glancing blow to the head. An ambulance was called to take John to hospital for emergency treatment. John was off work for three weeks while his sprained back settled down, but he still gets a reoccurring back twinge if he moves quickly and occasional bad headaches that the doctor has put down to the blow to his head.

■ Whose fault was the accident?

■ What actions do you think Kevin and John should have taken to avoid this accident?

key terms

Joist: one of a series of parallel beams that span the gap between walls in suspended floors and roofs, to support floor, ceiling and flat roof surfaces.

I've been told that manual handling is a major cause of workplace musculoskeletal disorders. What are they and how do they develop?

Musculoskeletal disorders or MSDs are those disorders that affect the joints, muscles, tendons, ligaments and nerves and include repetitive strain injuries. Most MSDs develop over time from years of moving heavy items, awkward or bulky shapes or using poor procedures and postures.

Safe lifting procedures

Where avoidance of manual handling is not reasonably practicable, the adoption of safe lifting procedures will reduce the potential risk of injury.

 ACTIVITY

Draw lines between the appropriate boxes to connect the two parts of the practical tips to be followed when lifting materials and equipment:

Get a good grip:	On a suitable platform, ensuring your hands and fingers will not be trapped, before sliding the load into position. Where the load has to be lowered to the floor level, you should adopt a similar position to that used when lifting.
Think first:	Always lift with your back straight, elbows tucked in, knees bent and feet slightly apart.
Place load down first:	Can I use an aid? Do I need help? What PPE is appropriate? Are there splinters, nails and sharp or jagged edges on the items to be moved?
Take up the correct position:	Avoiding any twisting and leaning, keeping the load close to your body and look straight ahead rather than down at the load.
Move smoothly:	Using your leg muscles and not your back.
Lift the load:	Hands should be placed under the load and, on lifting, the load should be hugged as close as possible to your body.

Handle materials and equipment

 ACTIVITY

State THREE checks to be made before manually moving materials from storage to the workplace to ensure the intended route is clear and safe:

1.

2.

3.

ACTIVITY

Number the following action points, which are aimed at minimising the amount of waste material in construction, to identify the correct order of priority:

- [ ] Dispose of waste in a landfill site.
- [ ] Eliminate waste wherever possible.
- [ ] Reuse materials that are potential waste.
- [ ] Reduce the amount of waste created.
- [ ] Recycle waste materials wherever possible.

Basic working platforms

Each year in the construction industry, numerous falls take place as a result of the use of working platforms and access equipment such as scaffolding and ladders. It is therefore of major importance that the risks of working at height are assessed and appropriate work equipment is selected and used.

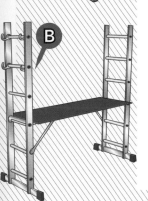

ACTIVITY

Look at the illustrations in the margin, which show a range of working platforms and access equipment. Name each item and describe a situation where each would be suitable to use:

A

B

C

Your questions answered...

Why can't I use a milk crate, saw stool or chair as a hop-up to gain access to low level work, which is just out of reach?

These should never be used as they are not designed for this purpose and may overturn or collapse completely, resulting in injury.

Stepladders

Stepladders are used mainly for short duration internal work on firm, flat surfaces and should be inspected on a daily basis by the person intending to use them.

 ACTIVITY

Produce a pre-use list of checks to be made before using stepladders:

Scaffolds

Scaffolding is a temporary structure that is used in order to carry out certain building operations at height. Tubular scaffolding and fittings is the most common type of scaffolding used in the construction industry to provide a safe means of access to heights and a safe working platform.

 ACTIVITY

Use the internet to research types of tubular scaffolding and complete the following tasks:

1. Name different types of tubular scaffolding.

2. State THREE requirements for a ladder that is used to provide access to the scaffold's working platform.

   1.

   2.

   3.

Your questions answered...

Is it OK if I temporarily remove part of a scaffold in order to make my work easier?

No, you must never remove any part of a scaffold as it can weaken it and you may be responsible for its total collapse. Scaffolding must only be erected, altered or dismantled by a trained, competent 'carded scaffolder'.

What is a 'carded scaffolder'?

A 'carded scaffolder' is a person who holds a recognised skills card or certificate showing that they have been trained and assessed as being competent in the erection, alteration, dismantling and inspection of tubular scaffolding.

Basic working platforms

ACTIVITY

List FOUR general visual checks that should be made before using a scaffold:

1.

2.

3.

4.

ACTIVITY

Using the internet or a textbook, look up the *Work at Height Regulations*. State THREE duties they place on employers and give reasons why:

1.

2.

3.

ACTIVITY

In a group consider these questions:

- What determines the maximum safe working height of a mobile tower scaffold?
- What is the maximum recommended load that can be carried up or down a ladder?
- What is the purpose of **handrails**, mesh guards and toe boards that are fitted to working platforms?

key terms

Handrail: a rail that is designed to provide a person with stability and support when using stairs and associated landings.

Working with electricity in a construction environment

Colour codes for different voltages

Electrical supply cables and industrial shielded plugs and sockets are colour coded to show their purpose and the voltage they are carrying.

ACTIVITY

Give the voltage and intended use of each of the colour codes:

Red:

Blue:

Yellow:

Your questions answered...

I've been told that my drill's battery charger must be PAT tested and receive a pass certificate before I can use it in the workplace. What is a PAT test and how often must it be carried out?

PAT is the abbreviation used for portable appliance testing. Under the Electricity at Work Regulations all portable electrical appliances used in the workplace have to be tested by a competent person at regular intervals, to ensure they are safe to use. PAT testing is normally carried out on an annual basis, but can be varied depending on the frequency of use.

Working with electricity

 ACTIVITY

In a small group, consider the following real-life problem or scenario:

Sanjay is a recently qualified carpenter who is undertaking refurbishment work for a specialist contractor.

While he was working on battening out walls and fixing a plasterboard lining, he had to cut out holes for electrical sockets and pull the cables through.

The electrician had taped over the exposed ends of the cables for protection; all was going well until there was a loud bang and sparks as Sanjay pulled the cables though the last box. Sanjay received an electric shock and burns to his fingers, which required hospital treatment and time off work.

- What do you think was the cause of Sanjay's accident?

- Whose fault was it?

- What precautions should Sanjay take in the future when working with or near electrical equipment?

 ACTIVITY

1. What voltage is specified when using portable electrical equipment on building sites?

2. Name the item of equipment that can be used to operate reduced voltage electrical equipment from a mains supply.

3. Explain why using reduced voltage electrical equipment is safer than using just a mains supply.

Using personal protective equipment (PPE) correctly

PPE

PPE is the equipment and clothes a worker needs to wear, or use, to protect them from risks to their health and safety that cannot be eliminated or adequately controlled in other ways. Not using PPE, or using inappropriate or damaged PPE, can cause injuries, ill-health and industrial diseases.

When choosing items of PPE, you should ask yourself the following questions:

➤ Is it the right item for the working conditions and the risks involved?

➤ Will it help to control the risks without adding to them?

➤ Can it be adjusted so that it fits correctly and is comfortable to use?

➤ Will you still be able to carry out your work task properly while wearing the item?

➤ If you need to use more than one item of PPE at the same time, are they compatible?

➤ Is the item well maintained and in good working order?

Types of PPE

ACTIVITY

Look at the photographs. Name each item and state a situation where it is required:

Your questions answered...

Is it safe to continue wearing a damaged item of PPE until it can be replaced?

No, as it will not provide adequate protection. Any items of PPE that have been damaged or show signs of wear must not be worn and should be replaced immediately before any further work is undertaken.

ACTIVITY

In the table below, explain for each of the following risks the appropriate actions to be followed and the PPE required:

Risk	Action and PPE
Skin cancer	
Cuts and infections	
Head injury	
Leptospirosis	
Hearing damage	

ACTIVITY

Name the items of PPE that are considered mandatory and should be worn onsite at all times:

ACTIVITY

You are working on a construction site and you notice someone wearing a dust mask but there are toxic fumes present. Why is this an incorrect use of PPE? What would you say to the person?

Fire and emergency procedures

Elements essential for a fire

The three essential elements that are required for a fire to ignite and burn are fuel, oxygen and heat or an ignition source.

 ACTIVITY

1. What is the name given to the illustration?

2. Explain what it represents.

3. What would be the result of removing one of the elements?

Methods of fire prevention

Employers should undertake a risk assessment of the workplace to establish the type and number of fire extinguishers required in the event of an emergency. Employers also have a duty to undertake certain actions in order to eliminate or reduce the risks in the workplace.

 ACTIVITY

List THREE potential fire hazards that should be taken into consideration during a risk assessment:

1.

2.

3.

Procedures in emergency situations

Emergencies are situations or events that require immediate action and it is essential that individuals are aware of the procedures and responsibilities for dealing with them.

ACTIVITY

List FIVE actions that members of the workforce should take in the event of a fire or other emergency situation arising:

1.

2.

3.

4.

5.

Types of fire extinguishers

There are various fire extinguishers and fire blankets available for tackling a fire in its early stages. It is essential that the correct type is selected, as using the wrong type can make the fire spread or cause injury to the user.

ACTIVITY

Look up the types of fire extinguisher on the web or in a textbook. Using the table below, state the content of each and what type of fire they are suitable to be used on.

Label colour	Content	Type of fire

Your questions answered...

Is it OK to go back into the building and help put out a fire after reporting to the assembly point?

No, the use of fire extinguishers should only be considered for small fires in their early stages or where the fire is blocking your escape route. Under no circumstances should you re-enter the site or building until the nominated person authorises it.

Safety signs and notices

Types of safety sign

A range of safety signs can be seen displayed around the workplace. Each has a designated shape, colour and symbol or pictogram to ensure that health and safety information is presented to employees in a consistent, standard way.

ACTIVITY

Look at the illustrations in the margin, which show the basic shapes and colours used for safety signs. Name and state the purpose of each sign:

Use of supplementary text safety signs

Although the purpose of a safety sign is identified by its designated shape, colour and symbol or pictogram, they are often supported by supplementary text to provide additional information and instruction.

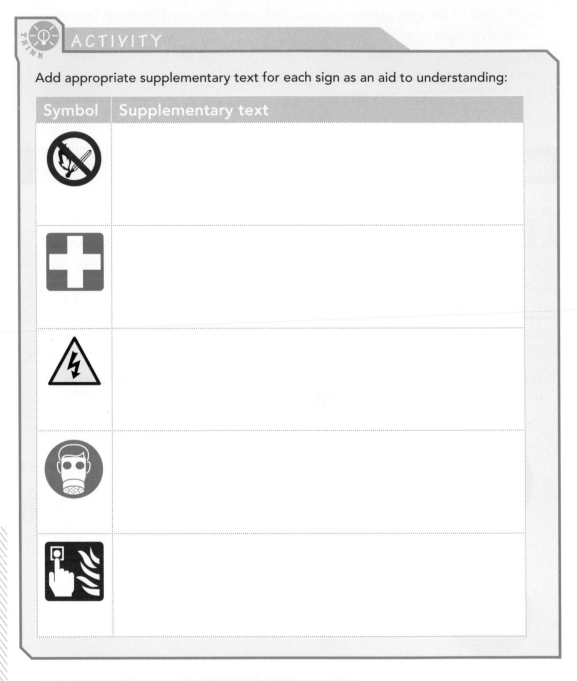

ACTIVITY

Add appropriate supplementary text for each sign as an aid to understanding:

Symbol	Supplementary text

Your questions answered...

What are hand signals used for?

A hand signal can be used to direct hazardous operations, such as crane and vehicle manoeuvres. Anyone giving hand signals must be competent, wear distinctive brightly-coloured (hi-viz) clothing and use the standard arm and hand movements.

Spot the hazards

ACTIVITY

Look at the illustration of an unsafe building site and identify safety hazards, breaches of regulations and general unsafe practices. Circle each one and number it – there are at least 10 but you may find more.

Describe each hazard in the following list.

1. ....
   ....
   ....

2. ....
   ....
   ....

3. ....
   ....
   ....

4. ....
   ....
   ....

5. ....
   ....
   ....

6. ....

7. ....

8. ....

9. ....

10. ....

QUICK QUIZ

1. Which one of the following abbreviations refers to the main legislation that deals with health and safety in all workplaces?
   a. COSHH
   b. HASAWA
   c. PUWER
   d. RIDDOR

2. Why is it important to report a near miss, even if no one is hurt?
   a. it should be recorded in the accident book
   b. lessons can be learned, which help to prevent future accidents
   c. you may be able to get compensation
   d. someone may have to be disciplined

3. What is the purpose of a safety sign that has a red circle and diagonal line on a white background?
   a. identifies fire equipment or where to find it
   b. indicates something that you must not do
   c. indicates something that you must do
   d. warns of a specific hazard

4. What is the principal cause of fatal accidents on construction sites?
   a. contact with moving machinery
   b. contact with electricity
   c. falls from a height
   d. struck by a falling object

5. Under the Health and Safety at Work Act, which one of the following is an employee's duty?
   a. ensure that equipment is safely designed
   b. prepare a safety policy
   c. use the equipment and safeguards provided
   d. provide and maintain a safe working environment

6. Which one of the following is not an employer's responsibility under the Health and Safety at Work Act?
   a. provide employees with the necessary information, instruction, training and supervision to ensure safe working
   b. provide employees with safe transportation to and from work
   c. provide and maintain a safe working environment
   d. ensure safe access to and from the workplace

7. Legislation is:
   a. something that only applies to employers
   b. a guide to explain best health and safety practices
   c. a law or set of laws that must be followed by all
   d. an approved code of practice that gives explanations of the law

8. Which one of the following regulations deals with the control of hazardous substances?
   a. PUWER
   b. COSHH
   c. RIDDOR
   d. PPER

9. A fire extinguisher containing water can be used on:
   a. Class A fires
   b. Class B fires
   c. Class C fires
   d. Class E fires

10. What colour is used in the workplace to denote that the equipment uses a 110 volt supply?
    a. red
    b. blue
    c. yellow
    d. black

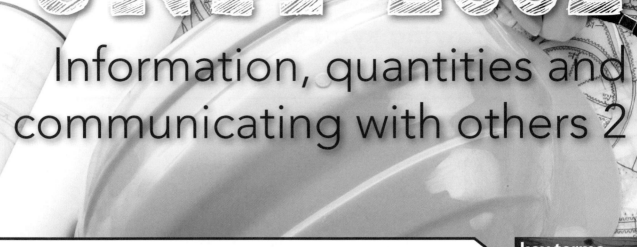

UNIT 2002

Information, quantities and communicating with others 2

Working in the construction industry involves working with, producing and interpreting a wide range of information to suit the needs of a project. At the same time, it involves working within a team and **communicating** effectively with other people.

Key knowledge:
➤ interpretation and production of building information
➤ estimating quantities of resources
➤ communicating workplace requirements efficiently.

key terms

Communicating: involves the exchange of thoughts, messages and information, by speech, body language, written or printed information and telecommunications.

Interpreting and producing building information

Drawing symbols

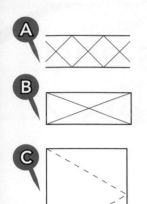

ACTIVITY

Look at the illustrations and describe what each drawing symbol represents:

A

B

C

D

Your questions answered...

Why have I been told by my supervisor not to scale off dimensions from a drawing?

Although scale rules can be useful when reading drawings, preference should always be given to written dimensions shown on a drawing. Mistakes can be made due to the dimensional instability of paper at differing moisture contents or where a fold in the paper might make it impossible to get an accurate size.

ACTIVITY

Using the following specifications, make a sketch or drawing to show a cross section through a two-storey domestic house and label all the parts.

- **Foundations:** Concrete strip.

- **External walls:** Cavity wall, comprising brick outer leaf, blockwork inner leaf, cavity wall insulation, damp proof course (DPC) and gypsum plaster to inner surfaces.

- **Ground floor:** Solid construction, comprising hardcore, blinding, damp proof membrane (DPM), concrete over-site, insulation and cement screed.

- **Upper floor:** Suspended timber construction, comprising timber joists supported on hangers, herringbone strutting, tongue and groove (T&G) floorboarding and plasterboard ceiling.

- **Roof:** Pitched construction with overhang eaves, comprising trussed rafters supported on wall plates, concrete roof tiles and ridge capping, tiling battens on sarking felt and plasterboard ceiling.

Using a scale rule

ACTIVITY

The outline ground floor plan of a house shown below is drawn to a scale of 1:100.

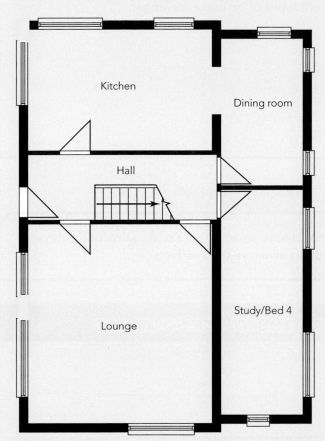

Use your scale rule to measure the lengths and then complete the table:

Room	Length	Width	Area
Lounge			
Dining room			
Kitchen			
Study/Bed 4			
Hall			

Interpreting and producing building information

ACTIVITY

Name and describe THREE different types of building drawings:

1.

2.

3.

ACTIVITY

In a group, discuss what factors could have an effect on the duration of a contract programme and what you could do to minimise these effects.

Estimating quantities of resources

Basic shapes

ACTIVITY

The table below illustrates a range of common shapes. Complete the table to show the formulae that can be used to calculate the area and perimeter of each shape.

Shape	Area	Perimeter
Square		
Rectangle		
Triangle		
Circle		

Estimating quantities of materials

ACTIVITY

Look at the illustration below, which shows a simple dimensioned sketch of a room in a domestic house:

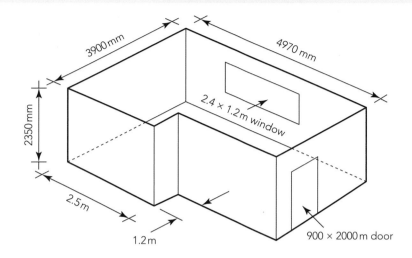

1. Calculate the amount of hardwood tongue and groove flooring required to overboard the floor, if the boards have a covering width of 65 mm.

2. Determine the minimum number of full 2400 × 1200 sheets of plasterboard required to dry line the walls of the room.

3. Calculate the total length of skirting required for the room.

4. Using the following information, determine the total cost of materials:

    ■ Tongue and groove boarding at £2.25 per metre.

    ■ Plasterboard at £10.20 per pair of boards.

    ■ Skirting at 95p per metre.

    ■ Allow 7.5 per cent for cutting and wastage on the flooring and skirting, plus an additional 5 per cent on the total material costs to cover consumable items.

Estimating quantities of resources

ACTIVITY

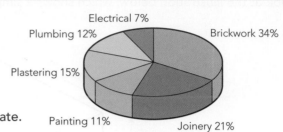

1. The pie chart shows the estimated costs for a building job, as a percentage of the total cost of £22,750. What is the estimated cost of the joinery?

   Electrical 7%
   Plumbing 12%
   Brickwork 34%
   Plastering 15%
   Painting 11%
   Joinery 21%

2. State the difference between a quotation and an estimate.

3. State TWO possible implications of inaccurate estimates.

   1.

   2.

Communicating workplace requirements efficiently

ACTIVITY

Look at the photographs and describe what you think the body language communicates:

A

B

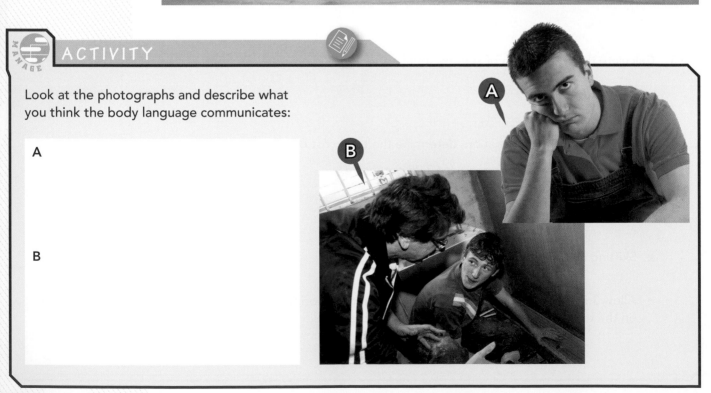

A

B

ACTIVITY

Match each type of meeting to its appropriate description:

Regular meetings	A one-to-one meeting between an employee and a line manager, often on an annual basis. These are used to discuss an employee's successes and failures, strengths and weaknesses, and their suitability for promotion or further training, etc.
A pre-start or 'kick-off' meeting	A meeting between the project manager, site foreman and sub-contractors held to discuss and resolve general site issues, including progress of work, reasons for delay, working together, site safety and security issues.
Weekly domestic meetings	A meeting involving the client team, design team and the construction team held to discuss progress made to date, problems or issues that have arisen since the last meeting and to table any amendments to drawings, specifications or other contract documents.
Informal meetings	A meeting involving the client team, design team and the construction team. It provides the opportunity for those involved to get to know each other, agree methods of communication and points of contact.
Performance review	A meeting called as and when required at short notice to discuss and resolve any urgent problems arising during the project that cannot wait until the next programmed meeting.

ACTIVITY

List THREE types of communication in the workplace, plus an advantage and disadvantage of each:

Type of communication	Advantage	Disadvantage

QUICK QUIZ

How much do you know about information, quantities and communicating with others?

1. Which one of the following documents contains written descriptions of the material quality and standards of workmanship for a particular contract?
   a. conditions of contract
   b. specification
   c. building regulations
   d. bill of quantities

2. Symbols are used on building drawings to:
   a. represent different materials and components
   b. indicate the company that designed the building
   c. brighten up a drawing
   d. avoid the use of long words

3. The purpose of a programme of work is to:
   a. show the hierarchy of the building team
   b. indicate when materials have to be ordered by
   c. show the order in which site operations are to be undertaken
   d. indicate the lines of communication

4. Site plan drawings are used to show:
   a. the proposed site in relation to the surrounding area
   b. the position of the proposed building in relation to roads, services and drainage
   c. the general layout of the proposed building
   d. the general layout of site accommodation and material storage

5. Block plans are often drawn using a scale of:
   a. 1:1 or 1:10
   b. 1:25 or 1:50
   c. 1:250 or 1:500
   d. 1:1250 or 1:2500

6. Range drawings are used to show:
   a. the basic sizes of standard components
   b. the information required to manufacture a component
   c. the general site layout
   d. the joints between various building elements

7. What does the abbreviation 'bdg' on a drawing refer to?
   a. building
   b. boarding
   c. binding
   d. brickwork

8. The person appointed to resolve disputes or conflicts between individual people or groups who can't agree is called a:
   a. communicator
   b. conciliator
   c. mediator
   d. judge

9. Details of all windows and associated ironmongery required for a particular job would be shown on a:
   a. specification
   b. variation order
   c. schedule
   d. confirmation notice

10. The most common form of communication between operatives working on the same site is via:
    a. text
    b. voice mail
    c. spoken word
    d. body language

UNIT 2003

Building methods and construction technology 2

There are many different types of buildings and structures required to fulfil the needs and expectations of today's ever-demanding society. The main examples are **residential**, **commercial** and **industrial** buildings and **facilities for transport**.

Collectively, these buildings and structures are known as the built environment, while individually they are known as elements of the built environment.

key terms

Residential: houses and flats, etc.
Commercial: shops and offices, etc.
Industrial: factories, workshops, mills and warehouses, etc.
Facilities for transport: roads, bridges, railways, harbours and airports, etc.

Key knowledge:
➤ principles behind walls, floors and roofs
➤ principles behind internal work
➤ delivery and storage of building materials.

Walls, floors and roofs

Types of foundations

ACTIVITY

Name FOUR different types of foundations and state a typical use for each.

	Name	Use
1.		
2.		
3.		
4.		

Types of wall

ACTIVITY

Produce sketches in the space below to show the difference between solid, cavity and framed external walls:

Roof structures

ACTIVITY

Describe the TWO methods of construction that may be used to form pitched roofs:

1.

2.

Principles behind walls, floors and roofs

ACTIVITY

Use the space below to explain the difference between the sub-structure and super-structure of a building.

Internal work

Effects of heat and fire on masonry, concrete, timber and metal

ACTIVITY

Building materials can be classed as either combustible or non-combustible; however, both types can be affected by heat and fire. Complete the table to describe the effect of heat and fire on a range of building materials.

Material	Effect of heat and fire
Bricks, blocks and stone	
Concrete	
Timber	
Metal	

Deterioration to masonry

ACTIVITY

Look at the photographs. Name the type of deterioration you can see and explain the cause.

A

B

C

Types, properties and use of glass

ACTIVITY

Look up the following types of glass by doing an internet search:

- Float glass
- Toughened glass
- Laminated glass
- Low E glass
- Self-cleaning glass

Using a computer, place each type of glass in a table. Add a description and an example of where each might be used.

Principles behind internal work

ACTIVITY

Under the headings below, state how the effect of fire can be minimised in timber and metal building materials:

- Timber

- Metal

Delivery and storage of building materials

 ACTIVITY

Look at the photographs. Name the type of equipment and state a typical use:

A

B

 ACTIVITY

Building materials can be destroyed by extremes of temperature, absorption of moisture and exposure to sunlight.

Complete the table to describe the correct storage requirements for a range of building materials.

Material	Storage requirements
Aggregates	
Bricks and blocks	
Carcassing timber	
Cement	
Flammable liquids	
Glass	
Metal	
Paint	
Thermal insulation	

ACTIVITY

List the checks that should be made when materials are delivered to construction sites:

Your questions answered...

I've been instructed by my foreman to keep the carcassing timber covered up to prevent it becoming damp, but what's the reason?

All timbers readily absorb and lose moisture to achieve a balance with their surroundings. However, this causes the timber to expand and shrink, which can cause it to distort, split and crack. Damp timber incorporated into new buildings will result in excessive shrinkage, opening up of joints and cracks between elements and components, such as wide gaps between floorboards and cracks between walls and ceiling line, etc. as it eventually dries out and shrinks. In addition, damp and wet timber is highly susceptible to biological attack.

Building methods wordsearch

ACTIVITY

Solve the clues and find the answers hidden in the word square.

You may find the words written forwards, backwards, up, down or diagonally.

Draw a ring around the words, or a line through them using a highlighter pen:

E	F	L	O	A	T	G	L	A	S	S	D	L	I
V	L	V	E	T	C	P	G	T	P	A	N	M	E
I	C	A	P	T	E	G	E	N	T	O	S	E	E
T	F	A	R	O	G	N	I	N	I	L	Y	R	D
A	G	E	O	R	I	I	L	S	E	P	P	E	C
V	D	S	F	T	F	R	S	E	P	G	P	L	I
R	N	E	I	P	N	E	P	T	T	D	O	A	F
E	F	F	L	O	R	E	S	C	E	N	C	E	C
S	N	S	E	P	R	N	V	G	R	P	I	S	L
R	S	L	M	L	L	I	B	L	D	O	P	L	G
E	I	O	E	R	P	G	R	O	O	A	R	E	T
P	C	E	G	A	K	N	I	R	H	S	F	E	D
E	F	A	C	I	S	E	C	O	N	D	A	R	Y
M	C	S	I	R	P	I	K	N	T	S	R	L	R

1. A paint used to form a protective coat against moisture and corrosion, or act as a barrier between dissimilar materials.
— — — — — — (6)

2. A sheet material that is formed by being floated on to the surface of liquid tin.
— — — — — / — — — — — (5&5)

3. Abbreviation for material used in walls to prevent the rise of moisture. — — — (3)

4. Used in walls to bridge openings.
— — — — — — (6)

5. Wall used to provide intermediate support to suspended ground floor joists.
— — — — — — — (7)

6. Process of applying plasterboard to a wall surface with dabs of adhesive.
— — — / — — — — — — (3&6)

7. Type of stress in the top of a structural beam under load.
— — — — — — — — — — — (11)

8. Strip foundation used for sloping ground.
— — — — — — — (7)

9. Foundation that covers the footprint of a building. — — — — (4)

10. Type of brick used to form a barrier against moisture movement.
— — — — — — — — — — — (11)

QUICK QUIZ

1. What is the main difference between bricklaying mortar and concrete?
   a. the amount of water used
   b. the type of aggregate used
   c. the type of cement used
   d. there is no difference between the two

2. Datum pegs and marks are where:
   a. all site levels are taken from
   b. the building line is set out from
   c. the walls of a building intersect
   d. stepped foundations are required

3. The type of foundation mainly used for low-rise domestic structures is:
   a. raft
   b. pile
   c. pad
   d. strip

4. What is the main difference between DPCs and DPMs?
   a. their purpose
   b. their location in a building
   c. the material they are made from
   d. there is no difference

5. The main purpose of bonding brickwork is to:
   a. provide a surface that plaster or rendering will bond to
   b. spread the loading evenly throughout the wall
   c. provide a decorative finished effect
   d. minimise the use of materials

6. Common rafters in a pitched roof are fixed at either end to:
   a. sole plate and purlin
   b. wall plate and ridge
   c. sole plate and crown
   d. wall plate and soffit board

7. What does the term 'galvanic protection' refer to?
   a. the painting of timber and metal to protect them from moisture
   b. the chemical treatment of steel and iron with zinc to prevent corrosion
   c. the pressure treatment of timber with a fire-retarding solution, that when heated gives off a vapour that will not burn
   d. the treatment of walls with a chemical to increase their moisture resistance

8. The type of bonding used in cavity walls is known as:
   a. cavity bond
   b. English bond
   c. stretcher bond
   d. Flemish bond

9. Phased deliveries of building materials in accordance with the programme will:
   a. increase costs
   b. reduce costs
   c. increase storage requirements
   d. reduce storage requirements

10. What type of subsoil is most likely to be affected by seasonal moisture changes?
   a. rock
   b. gravel
   c. clay
   d. sand

UNIT 2008

Carry out first fixing operations

First fixing is the carpentry work carried out after **carcassing** but before the building is plastered.

Key knowledge:
- ➤ fixing frames and linings including window frames
- ➤ fitting and fixing floor coverings and flat roof decking
- ➤ erecting timber stud partitions
- ➤ assembling, erecting and fixing straight flights of stairs including handrails.

key terms

Carcassing: the process of building the main carcass or skeleton of a building. With regard to carpentry and joinery, it consists of flooring and roofing. It is also used to describe the installation of pipework and ducts for services.

Fixing frames and linings

ACTIVITY

Look at the illustrations and name each type of frame or lining:

  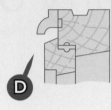

A

B

C

D

ACTIVITY

1. Explain the difference between 'built-in' and 'fixed-in' frames and state where each might be used.

2. Name THREE methods of securing the jambs of 'fixed-in' frames or linings.

3. Name the joint between the head and jamb of an external frame, illustrated in the margin. Explain the reason why the horn has been cut back.

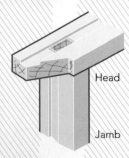

Head

Jamb

ACTIVITY

Produce a list of FIVE tools and items of equipment that you would include in your toolkit when fixing **door frames and linings**.

1.

2.

3.

4.

5.

Fitting and fixing floor coverings and flat roof decking

ACTIVITY

Look at the illustrations, which show a range of floorboards. Describe each and indicate whether it would be surface or secret fixed.

	Description	Surface fixed	Secret fixed

Forming access traps

Produce sketches in the space below to show the following:

1. How a tongue and groove floorboard over a water pipe notched across the top of joists can be made easily removable for later access.

2. How an access trap in a chipboard floor covering can be formed and supported between the joists.

Fitting and fixing floor coverings

1. Explain why heading joints in softwood floorboarding should be staggered throughout the floor.

2. Explain why a gap is left between floor coverings and walls.

3. State the reason for applying glue to the tongues and grooves of sheet floor covering prior to fixing.

Erecting timber stud partitions

Components and materials

ACTIVITY

Look at the illustration below, which shows the plan and elevation of a stud partition, and complete the tasks:

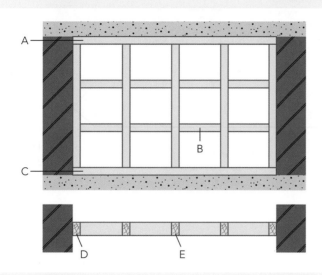

1. Name the component parts:

   A

   B

   C

   D

   E

2. Name a suitable timber and typical sectional size.

Your questions answered...

I know that plasterboard is available with either square edges for skimming or with tapered edges for use as a dry lining. However, I've just seen plasterboard with red/pink and green tinted cores. What are these used for?

Plasterboard with a red/pink tinted core is a fire-resistant board used where increased fire resistance is required, such as party walls. Plasterboard with a green tinted core is a moisture-resistant board used in areas subjected to moisture, such as kitchens and bathrooms. (This is the same colour coding that is used with other sheet material such as MDF and chipboard.)

Arrangement of members

ACTIVITY

Produce sectional sketches in the space below to show the arrangement of stud **partition** members at positions A, B and C:

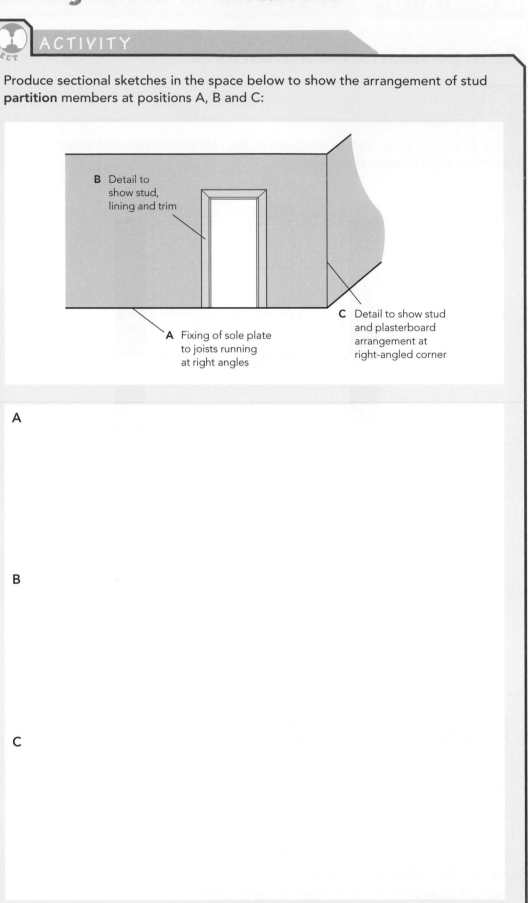

B Detail to show stud, lining and trim

A Fixing of sole plate to joists running at right angles

C Detail to show stud and plasterboard arrangement at right-angled corner

A

B

C

Erecting stud partitions

ACTIVITY

1. Describe a method of protecting services routed through a stud partition from the risk of later nail or screw damage.

2. State the purpose of noggins.

3. 'CLS' has been specified for making a stud partition. Explain what the abbreviation means and state an advantage of using it over sawn sections.

Assembling, erecting and fixing straight flights of stairs including handrails

ACTIVITY

Look at the illustrations and describe each type of stair.

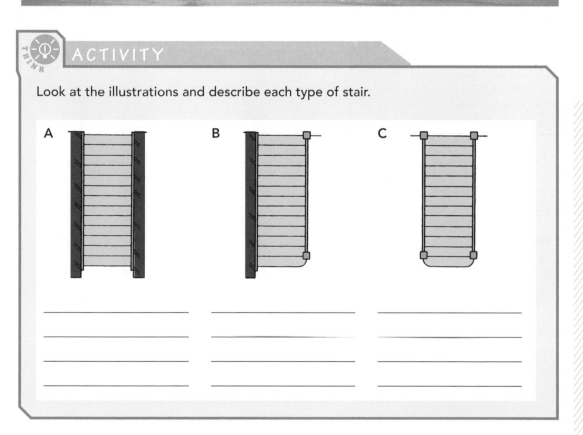

A _____

_____

_____

_____

B _____

_____

_____

_____

C _____

_____

_____

_____

ACTIVITY

Look at this illustration of a typical **flight of stairs**. Complete the labels and answer the questions.

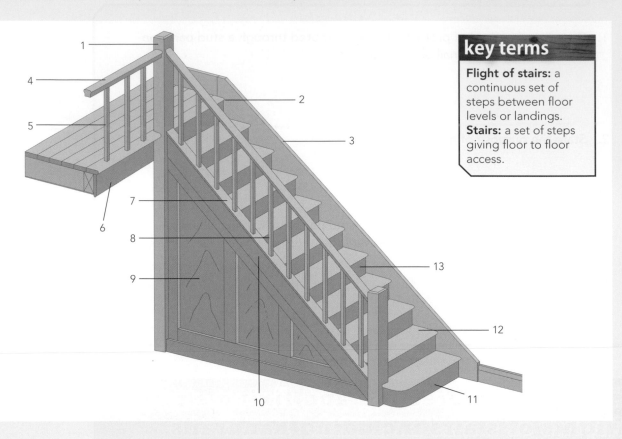

key terms

Flight of stairs: a continuous set of steps between floor levels or landings.
Stairs: a set of steps giving floor to floor access.

1. _____
2. _____
3. _____
4. _____
5. _____
6. _____
7. _____

8. _____
9. _____
10. _____
11. _____
12. _____
13. _____

1. Name the type of **stairs**.

2. State the regulations that apply to any gaps to the side of a stair or landing.

ACTIVITY

1. Name the joint used between the string and newel post and state how the shoulder is drawn up during site assembly.

2. State how the upper and lower newels can be secured at floor level.

3. Explain the purpose of using glue blocks on the underside of a stair between the tread and riser.

First fixing definitions

ACTIVITY

Match each first fixing term to its appropriate description.

Noggin	Horizontal piece of timber that is fixed between studs or joists to provide a fixing point or support the covering material.
Jamb	Inclined board into which the treads and risers are housed or cut.
Horn	Projection of the mortised member of a timber framework beyond the mortise.
String	Horizontal board fixed internally at sill level.
Stud	Outer vertical member of door frames and window frames.
Transom	Vertical member of a partition.
Apron lining	Boards used to finish the edge of a trimmed opening in a floor.
Window board	Intermediate horizontal member of a door frame or window frame.

QUICK QUIZ

How much do you know about carrying out first fixing operations?

1. The purpose of using heading joints in timber tongue and groove floorboarding is to:
   a. provide access to services
   b. enable cleaning of underfloor space
   c. utilise short lengths of board
   d. straighten bowed boards

2. The correct fixing device to secure an ex. 25 × 50 mm timber batten to the face of a proprietary plasterboard partition is a:
   a. toggle anchor
   b. framing anchor
   c. fibre wall plug
   d. timber connector

3. The component that is used to finish the top step of a flight of timber stairs is known as a:
   a. lining
   b. nosing
   c. capping
   d. architrave

4. The going of a step is measured from the:
   a. edge of one nosing to the edge of the next
   b. edge of one nosing to the face of the riser
   c. face of one riser to the back of the next
   d. face of one tread to the edge of the nosing

5. Square-edged flooring-grade chipboard must be:
   a. supported on all four edges
   b. supported on the short ends
   c. conditioned before fixing
   d. fixed with 10 mm gaps between each sheet

6. The vertical in-fill members of a staircase between the handrail and string are termed:
   a. spandrels
   b. newels
   c. balusters
   d. balustrades

7. Which one of the following statements is false?
   a. 18 mm chipboard is commonly used as a floor covering material
   b. screws and plugs can be used to fix replacement window frames in masonry wall openings
   c. tapered edge plasterboard is best for a taped and filled dry finish
   d. access traps in boarded floors should be well nailed to keep them secure

8. When fixing window boards, the front to back level is best checked using a:
   a. laser level
   b. long spirit level
   c. short spirit or boat level
   d. water level

9. What is the component that is temporarily fixed to a door frame or lining to maintain width and keep the jambs parallel while it is being fixed?
   a. strut
   b. tie piece
   c. brace
   d. distance piece

10. Which one of the following nail lengths is the most suitable for surface fixing 19 mm softwood floorboards?
    a. 38 mm
    b. 50 mm
    c. 62 mm
    d. 75 mm

UNIT 2009

Carry out second fixing operations

Second fixing is the work undertaken by the carpenter after the building has been made watertight and plastered or dry lined. Second fixing includes the hanging of doors, fitting of ironmongery, installation of moulded trim and the boxing out or encasement of services.

Key knowledge:
- ➤ installing side hung doors and ironmongery
- ➤ installing mouldings
- ➤ installing service encasements and cladding
- ➤ installing wall and floor units and fitments.

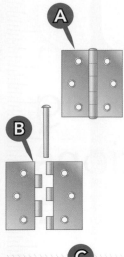

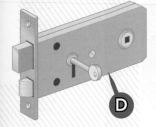

Installing side hung doors and ironmongery

ACTIVITY

Look at the illustrations in the margin and name the items of door ironmongery:

A

B

C

D

ACTIVITY

List the TEN tools and items of equipment that you would include in your toolkit when installing doors and ironmongery:

1.

2.

3.

4.

5.

6.

7.

8.

9.

10.

ACTIVITY

Read the following statements, research if necessary and place a tick in the appropriate boxes:

Material	True	False
The standard size for an internal door is 762 × 1981 × 35 mm.		
The outside vertical member of a panel door is called a jamb.		
A half-hour fire door with smoke seals may be labelled as FD30s.		
Solid core flush doors are normally considered to be of a better quality than hollow core flush doors.		
35 mm thick press MDF panel hollow core doors are for internal use.		
Tee hinges used to hang a ledged and braced door should be positioned so that they are on the same side as the upper ends of the braces.		
Horizontal mortise lock/latches are not suitable for narrow doors.		

ACTIVITY

In groups, consider what you know about installing side hung doors and ironmongery. Answer the following questions:

■ Why are internal doors normally 35 mm thick, but this is increased to 44 mm for external doors and half-hour fire doors?

■ How is the 'lock block' position on a hollow core door identified?

■ When fitting ironmongery, why may steel screws be initially used and then later replaced with brass screws?

■ What is the purpose of door and ironmongery schedules?

■ What does the term 'arris' mean and why should it be removed from door edges?

Installing mouldings

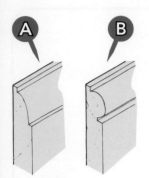

Identify mouldings

ACTIVITY

Look at the illustrations in the margin and name the moulding profiles:

A

B

C

Installing mouldings to an internal datum

ACTIVITY

The specification for a building states that the dado and picture rails in the ground floor rooms are to be fixed at a set distance above the internal datum. The internal datum has been marked by the site foreman in one position on the wall at 1m above FFL.

1. What does the abbreviation FFL mean?

2. How is the datum transferred to other positions in the building?

3. How is a level line marked around a wall at the correct height in order to fix the dado and picture rails?

Sequence of installing mouldings and hanging doors

ACTIVITY

Either in a small group or on your own, consider the following real-life problem or scenario:

Karen and Jade work for a small joinery company that mainly manufactures and installs joinery fitments.

However, they have been given the job of undertaking the second fixing to a two-room, ground-floor extension of a domestic house, which is a task that they have not undertaken before.

Karen suggests that it would be easier to fit the skirting and architrave before hanging the doors as the space will be less cluttered.

- What do you think of Karen's suggestion?
- What are the potential implications?
- What is the normal sequence of undertaking second fixing?

Your questions answered...

Why are scribes normally used for the internal corners of skirting board and not mitres?

Scribing is the preferred method as wall corners are rarely perfectly square, making the fitting difficult and, in addition, mitres will open up as a result of any shrinkage, showing a much larger gap than scribes.

ACTIVITY

Name THREE materials that are used for mouldings and trim:

1.

2.

3.

Installing service encasements and cladding

ACTIVITY

Look at the illustrations and answer the following questions:

1. Explain why the corner pipe casing in 'A' has been made using ladder frames.

2. State the purpose of using a plastic or metal corner trim in 'B'.

3. Explain why the lower panel of the pipe casing in 'C' has been formed in two pieces.

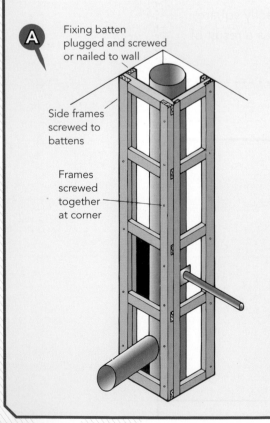

A Fixing batten plugged and screwed or nailed to wall

Side frames screwed to battens

Frames screwed together at corner

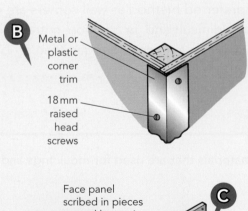

B Metal or plastic corner trim

18 mm raised head screws

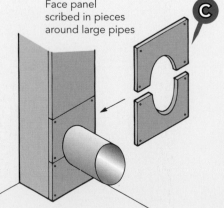

C Face panel scribed in pieces around large pipes

ACTIVITY

Produce labelled sketches in the space below to show the following details:

1. A skirting height pipe casing with an overhanging shelf.

2. How vee jointed matchboarding can be secret fixed to the grounds.

ACTIVITY

Use the space below to explain the purpose of encasing services:

Installing wall, floor units and fitments

Identify types of worktop

ACTIVITY

Look at the illustrations and name or describe each type of worktop:

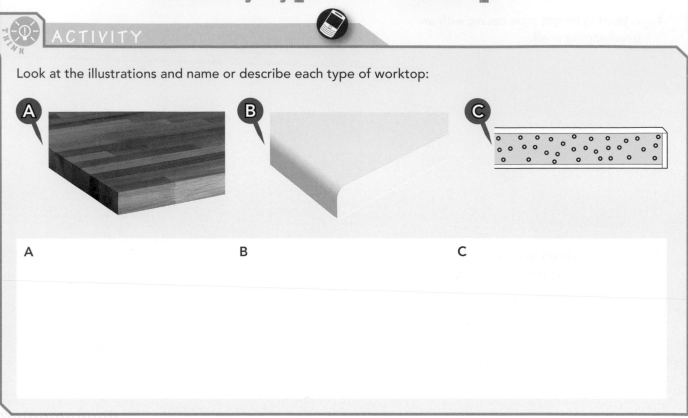

A	B	C

Your questions answered...

What is the difference between a fitment and an item of furniture?

Fitments are fixed or secured in some way to the structure, whereas items of furniture are normally freestanding.

ACTIVITY

Name TWO methods of jointing 'post-formed' worktops at internal corner returns:

1.

2.

Installing kitchen units

ACTIVITY

Name THREE materials that can be used to manufacture 'boxed' units:

1.

2.

3.

ACTIVITY

Look at the floor plan and elevations of a kitchen to be fitted. Answer the following questions.

1. Describe the procedure to be followed for the assembly of a 'flat pack' base unit, up to the stage when it is ready to be installed.

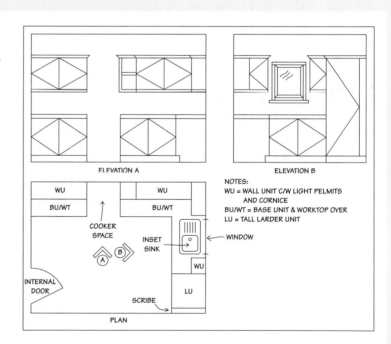

2. State how the intended hanging sides of the doors are indicated in the elevations.

3. State how the hole for the inset sink may be marked out and cut into the worktop.

Second fixing wordsearch

ACTIVITY

Solve the following clues and find the answers hidden in the word square.
You may find the words written forwards, backwards, up, down or diagonally.
Draw a ring around the words, or a line through them using a highlighter pen.

1. The documents used to record repetitive design information.
   _ _ _ _ _ _ _ _ _ (9)

2. The process of cutting the edge of an architrave to fit the wall contour.
   _ _ _ _ _ _ _ _ (8)

3. Saw cuts in the rear face of trim that is to be fixed to a curved surface.
   _ _ _ _ _ _ _ (7)

4. Used to ease fixing problems when skirting is thicker than architrave.
   _ _ _ _ _ _ /_ _ _ _ _ (6&5)

5. Applied to the edge of doors. _ _ _ _ _ _ _ /_ _ _ _ (7&4)

6. Groove adjacent to a mould. _ _ _ _ _ (5)

7. Distance between edge of door lining and architrave. _ _ _ _ _ _ (6)

8. The extending material at both ends of a door stile. _ _ _ _ _ (5)

9. Sharp corner on a timber section. _ _ _ _ _ (5)

10. An item of PPE worn onsite at all times.
    _ _ _ _ _ _ /_ _ _ _ _ _ (6&6)

H	L	P	L	C	M	L	Q	H	L	R	M
R	R	G	R	Q	G	N	P	T	R	E	R
E	S	C	H	E	D	U	L	E	S	N	S
N	E	G	D	E	G	N	I	D	A	E	L
K	S	C	R	I	B	I	N	G	S	M	R
T	E	M	L	E	H	Y	T	E	F	A	S
S	C	R	O	S	K	K	H	H	R	R	I
N	T	O	F	D	R	S	B	O	E	G	R
L	H	N	G	I	S	A	L	T	R	I	R
D	I	A	U	R	N	L	O	H	B	N	A
I	G	Q	T	G	S	G	C	E	I	S	S
I	C	H	H	H	C	E	K	B	U	E	E

QUICK QUIZ

1. The normal sequence for undertaking second fixing is:
   a. doors, skirting, architrave
   b. doors, architrave, skirting
   c. architrave, doors, skirting
   d. skirting, doors, architrave

2. The hand of a particular door can be found by reference to a:
   a. door schedule
   b. floor plan
   c. specification
   d. range drawing

3. Which of the following types of door is a five-lever mortise deadlock most likely to be used for?
   a. an internal living room door
   b. a bathroom door
   c. an external front entrance door
   d. an adult's bedroom door

3. The normal thickness of internal doors, external doors and half-hour fire doors is:
   a. 25 mm, 35 mm and 44 mm respectively
   b. 35 mm, 44 mm and 44 mm respectively
   c. 35 mm, 44 mm and 54 mm respectively
   d. 35 mm, 35 mm and 44 mm respectively

4. The reason for boring a spindle hole for a latch from both sides of the door is:
   a. the drill is too short to bore all the way
   b. to provide greater accuracy
   c. to prevent break out
   d. it is easier to mark out

5. The purpose of fixing architraves around a door opening is to:
   a. strengthen a thin door lining
   b. cover the joint
   c. help fix the lining or frame to the wall
   d. provide a straight line for the plasterer

6. The external corners of skirting are best:
   a. butted
   b. scribed
   c. mitred
   d. tongued

7. The best concealed method of fixing softwood matchboard panelling is to:
   a. secret nail through the tongue
   b. screw through the face and conceal heads with matching cover caps
   c. use secret headed nails or screws through the face of the board
   d. nail through the face, punch heads below the surface and fill the hole

8. Which one of the following statements is incorrect?
   a. water pipe casings located in living rooms may be filled with insulation material to protect the pipes from freezing.
   b. access panels in pipe casings can be surface screwed in position using cups and screws.
   c. ladder frames are required for casings, where a thin covering material is used.
   d. the use of WBP plywood is recommended for casings in wet areas, such as bathrooms

9. When cutting a butt and mitred joint on post-formed worktop returns it is best to use a:
   a. plunge action circular saw
   b. jig saw and template
   c. fine point panel saw
   d. router and template

10. Which one of the following is the best way to fix units to a timber stud partition wall?
    a. screw into any studs that can be located
    b. screw into pre-positioned noggins
    c. use plastic toggle fixings and screws
    d. use plasterboard screws

UNIT 2010

Erect structural carcassing

Carcassing is the process of building the main carcass or skeleton of a building. With regards to carpentry and joinery, this consists of flooring and roofing. It is also used to describe the installation of pipework and ducts for services.

Key knowledge:
- ➤ erecting trussed rafter roofs
- ➤ constructing gables, verge and eaves
- ➤ installing floor joists.

Erecting trussed rafter roofs

Proprietary fixings

ACTIVITY

Look at the photographs. Name the proprietary fixings and state a typical use of each:

A

B

C

Procedure for erecting trussed rafter roofs

ACTIVITY

Produce a list in working order to show the main stages in the erection of a **trussed rafter** roof:

1.

2.

3.

4.

5.

6.

7.

8.

9.

10.

key terms

Trussed rafter: a prefabricated roofing component consisting of a pair of rafters, ceiling tie/joist and struts, which are joined at their intersections with galvanised metal gang nail or pressed plates.

Erecting trussed rafter roofs

ACTIVITY

1. Explain how trussed rafters should be carried and manually positioned.

2. Explain the purpose of lateral restraint straps in roofing structures.

3. State the advantages of using trussed rafters over a traditional cut-rafter roof.

Your questions answered...

What is the purpose of using complete pre-assembled and weatherproofed trussed rafter roof structures?

This method creates a weatherproof structure more quickly than assembling the roof in situ. It also has potential health and safety benefits due to the workforce not having to undertake all of the work at height.

Constructing gables, verge and eaves

ACTIVITY

Look at the illustrations in the margin and name each roof shape:

A

B

C

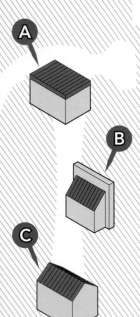

 ACTIVITY

Read the following statements and place a tick in the appropriate boxes:

Material	True	False
The **verge** is the lowest part of a roof where the rafters overhang the wall.		
Cradling brackets are used to support the soffit board of open overhanging **eaves**.		
Sprocket pieces reduce the pitch of the roof at the eaves.		
Plastic (uPVC) fascias and soffits are usually fixed with plastic headed stainless steel ring shank nails.		
Angle or tilting fillets used in felt-covered flat roofs help prevent the felt cracking.		

 ACTIVITY

In the space below, produce sketches to illustrate the following methods of finishing the eaves of a pitched roof:

Flush eaves

Open eaves

Closed eaves

key terms

Gable: the triangular portion of the end wall of a building with a pitched roof.

Verge: the termination or edge of a pitched roof at a gable or the sloping non-drained edge of a flat roof.

Eaves: the lower edge of a roof, which overhangs the walls and where the rainwater is discharged, normally into a gutter.

Replacing sash cords

ACTIVITY

In a small group consider the answers to the following questions.

- What piece of equipment can be attached to the end of a sash cord to aid its feeding over the pulley?

- Why it is recommended to replace all four sash cords at the same time rather than just the broken one?

- Why is it important to return weights to their original positions when replacing sash cords?

- Describe how the weights in a boxed sash window are accessed.

- Explain how sash cords are secured to the weight and sash stile.

Making good plaster, paintwork and brickwork

Your questions answered...

What's the difference between 'browning', 'bonding' and 'finish' plasters?

They are all gypsum-based plasters.

'Browning' and 'bonding' are used as a backing coat to walls and are applied in typically 10 mm thick layers: browning is used on absorbent surfaces such as common brickwork and building blocks; bonding is used on dense, less absorbent surfaces such as concrete, engineering bricks and surfaces coated in a PVA sealer. Another backing plaster available is 'hardwall', which has a higher impact resistance and a quicker drying surface.

'Finish' plaster is a skim coat applied over a backing coat to finish a wall surface with a typically 2 mm thick layer. Board finish plaster is available for skimming over plasterboard wall and ceiling surfaces, which has an additive that bonds to the plasterboard surface. There is also available a 'multi-finish' plaster that can be applied over the top of either browning or bonding backing coats or over plasterboard.

ACTIVITY

1. Describe a typical paint system for a bare softwood external door that has been replaced during maintenance operations.

2. Describe the preparation of a damaged blockwork wall surface before making patch plaster repairs.

3. State a mortar mix that is suitable for use when making brickwork repairs during the replacement of an external door frame.

4. Explain why the surface of backing plaster is scratched with a comb or scarifier before it has completely set.

Maintenance: true or false

ACTIVITY

Read the following statements and tick the appropriate boxes:

Statement	True	False
Pressure methods of applying timber preservative give a deeper penetration and are less prone to leaching out.		
Capillarity refers to the ability of water to travel against the force of gravity in fine spaces.		
Brickwork joints are often given a concave 'bucket handle' finish.		
The presence of flight holes in timber is the first stage of an attack by wood-boring insects.		
Lime may be added to a mortar mix to improve its workability.		
Parting beads must be removed before the bottom sash of a boxed-frame sash window can be taken out of the frame for repair and re-cording.		
The purpose of a wood primer is to seal the surface and provide a bond for later coats.		
Plasterers use hawks, trowels, rules and combs in their work.		
Hopper heads may be used at the lower end of a rainwater pipe to ease the flow of rainwater into an open gully.		
Rendering is a sand and cement mix that can be applied to weatherproof external walls.		

QUICK QUIZ How much do you know about carrying out maintenance?

1. Which one of the following components is fitted to a RWP to direct the flow of rainwater into an open grated gully?
   a. outlet
   b. hopper
   c. offset
   d. shoe

2. Which of the following conditions are required for an attack of dry rot?
   a. damp timber in excess of 20 per cent moisture content and good ventilation
   b. dry timber with moisture content of less than 20 per cent and bad or non-existent ventilation
   c. dry timber with moisture content of less than 20 per cent and good ventilation
   d. damp timber in excess of 20 per cent moisture content and bad or non-existent ventilation

3. The component part of a boxed-frame sash window that separates the sliding sash weights is the:
   a. staff bead
   b. wagtail
   c. sash bead
   d. parting bead

4. Which one of the following statements is false?
   a. the rebates of a glazed door should be primed before re-glazing
   b. painting of a replaced external door should not be undertaken in strong sunlight
   c. bonding in brickwork refers to the staggering of the horizontal joints
   d. the process of ruling off is associated with plastering

5. Access to the weights of a sliding sash window is achieved by removing the:
   a. upper and lower sashes
   b. pockets
   c. wagtails
   d. parting beads

6. On lifting a floorboard of a suspended ground floor there is a musty smell and the joists are found to be dry, powdery and easily crumbled. The most likely cause is:
   a. wet rot attack
   b. dry rot attack
   c. previous fire damage
   d. wood-boring insects

7. De-nibbing is a painting term related to which one of the following operations?
   a. filling surface to mask defects
   b. sealing the surface of knots
   c. rubbing down surface between coats
   d. wiping off surface with a 'low tack' cloth

8. A mortar mix for maintenance work has been specified with a ratio of 1:6, which means it has:
   a. 1 part water to 6 parts sand and sufficient cement to make it workable
   b. 1 part cement to 6 parts sand and sufficient water to make it workable
   c. 1 part cement to 6 parts water and sufficient sand to make it workable
   d. 1 part sand to 6 parts cement and sufficient water to make it workable

9. Replacement guttering and rainwater pipes are commonly made from:
   a. steel (galvanised)
   b. plastic (uPVC)
   c. timber (softwood)
   d. cement fibre

10. What is the purpose of coating damaged wall areas with a PVA bonding agent before undertaking repairs to plaster or rendering?
    a. it saves having to remove the loose plaster or rendering
    b. it provides a waterproof finish to the plaster or rendering
    c. it provides good adhesion between the plaster or rendering
    d. it enables a drier mix of plaster or rendering to be used

UNIT 2012

Set up and operate a circular saw

The extent to which carpenters and joiners are expected to use circular saws and other woodworking machines varies widely from firm to firm. There are many firms where the operation of any machine is exclusively the province of the trained machinist, and others where carpenters and joiners carry out all the machining. Also, there are the firms that fall between these two extremes, where machinists carry out bulk work but the joiners have at their disposal a limited range of machines for the occasional one-off job or replacement member.

Key knowledge:
➤ setting up fixed and transportable circular saws
➤ changing saw blades
➤ cutting timber and sheet material.

QUICK QUIZ — How much do you know about how to set up and operate a circular saw?

1. Which one of the following pieces of legislation specifically covers woodworking machines?
   a. CDM
   b. PUWER
   c. RIDDOR
   d. HASAWA

2. An extension or take-off table must be fitted to the rear of a circular saw bench. The minimum length measured from the saw spindle to the end of the table is:
   a. 800 mm
   b. 1000 mm
   c. 1200 mm
   d. 1400 mm

3. The arc on the fence of a circular saw bench should be adjusted so that it is:
   a. in line with the gullets of the blade's teeth
   b. in line with the blade's spindle
   c. set forward of the blade
   d. set beyond the blade

4. The conversion on a circular saw bench of a 50 × 200 mm timber section into two pieces of approximately 22 × 200 mm in section, is known as:
   a. facing
   b. edging
   c. flatting
   d. deeping

5. The minimum diameter saw blade that can be used on a circular sawing machine designed to accept a 600 mm maximum diameter saw blade is:
   a. 300 mm
   b. 360 mm
   c. 450 mm
   d. 600 mm

6. The guard on a circular saw that covers the saw blade is known as the:
   a. top guard
   b. extension guard
   c. crown guard
   d. shaw guard

7. The purpose of extraction fitted to circular saws is to reduce the:
   a. amount of air pollution
   b. number of accidents
   c. level of noise pollution
   d. amount of waste material

8. Practical guidance on the safe use of woodworking machinery can be found in an ACoP. What does ACoP stand for?
   a. approved common procedures
   b. alternative code of practice
   c. approved code of practice
   d. approved code of procedures

9. The purpose of the 300 mm yellow hatched area marked on the table of a cross-cut saw either side of the blade is:
   a. the minimum length of off-cut allowed
   b. to identify the 'no hands' area
   c. where off-cuts may be stored
   d. for training purposes only

10. The best method of timber conversion for joinery purposes is:
    a. rip sawn
    b. tangential sawn
    c. through and through
    d. quarter sawn

UNIT 2034

Produce setting-out details for routine joinery products

A large proportion of joinery used in the building industry today is **mass-produced** and is available **off-the-shelf**. However, mass-produced items are not always suitable and there is still a need to produce **purpose-made** joinery items for high-quality work, repairs and replacements, and one-off items to individual designs.

Before making anything but the most simple, one-off item of joinery, it is normal practice to set out a workshop rod and produce an accompanying cutting list. Setting out is done by the **setter-out**, who will translate the architect's scale details, specifications and their own survey details into full-size vertical and horizontal sections of the item. In addition, particularly where shaped work is concerned, elevations may also be required.

Key knowledge:

➤ interpreting information for setting out
➤ selecting resources for setting out
➤ setting out for bench joinery and site carpentry.

key terms

Mass-produced: joinery items produced in large quantities, using standard designs and sizes.

Off-the-shelf: standard joinery items that are readily available from a supplier.

Purpose-made: joinery items that are designed and manufactured for a specific purpose, normally in limited quantities and to specific designs and sizes.

Setter-out: an experienced bench joiner who is responsible for producing setting-out details for joinery items.

Interpreting information for setting out

Information sources

ACTIVITY

Before commencing setting out it is essential that you check all the drawings with the drawing register to ensure you are using the latest revisions.

Look at the illustrations below and name each type of drawing:

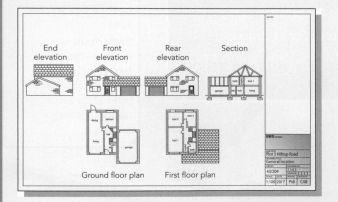

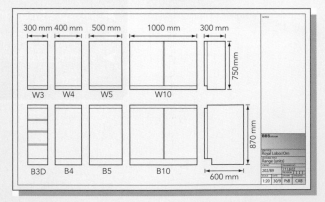

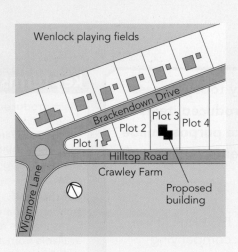

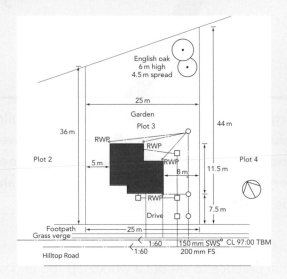

Specifications

ACTIVITY

Produce a sketch in the space below to show a window sill section that is described in a **specification** as three-times grooved, once chamfered, rebated, throated, weathered and pencil-rounded.

Building regulations

ACTIVITY

In groups of three, visit the planning portal website (www.planningportal.gov.uk) and look up the relevant **approved documents** (AD) with regards to a flight of stairs in a domestic house. Each of you explain one of the requirements for the following:

- Pitch of the stairs.
- Rise and going of a step.
- Gaps in a balustrade.

Your questions answered...

Why are workshop rods drawn full-size and not to a scale?

Rods are drawn full-size so that each component can be laid on the setting out so that critical lines can be transferred and marked out directly. Marking out from a scale drawing involves measuring each component individually, making allowances for joints and sectional profiles, etc., which is less accurate, can lead to inconsistencies in repeated items and is more time-consuming.

Why are workshop rods that are produced on paper considered to be less desirable?

Although paper rods are often considered more convenient because of their ease in handling and storage, they are less accurate in their use. This is because paper is more susceptible to dimension changes as a result of humidity and the inevitable creasing and folding of the paper, which can result in costly mistakes.

Interpreting information for setting out

ACTIVITY

1. What is the purpose of a workshop rod?

2. Explain the course of action required if you notice discrepancies in the information you have been given to set out from.

3. Define the work role of a joinery 'setter-out'.

Selecting resources for setting out

Types of timber

Timber can generally be divided into hardwoods and softwoods. Remember, this is based on their cellular structure and botanical grouping, not whether they are hard or soft.

 ACTIVITY

Apart from their cellular structure, state THREE main differences between hardwood and softwood trees:

1.

2.

3.

 ACTIVITY

In the table below, arrange the following timbers under the correct headings:

Oak   Redwood

Spruce   Maple

Douglas fir Elm

Mahogany   Ash

Beech

Hardwoods	Softwoods

Timber defects

Timber must be correctly converted, seasoned and preservative treated prior to use and regularly maintained to avoid one or more of the following types of defect:

➤ Natural defects.

➤ Processing/seasoning defects.

➤ Biological attack.

ACTIVITY

Look at the illustrations below. Complete the table to name and explain the type and cause of the timber defects shown:

Name	Type	Cause
A		
B		
C		
D		

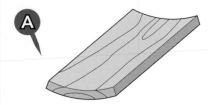

A

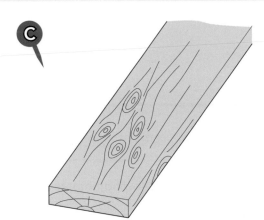

C

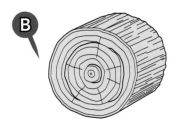

B

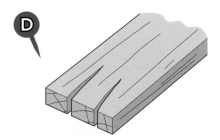

D

Your questions answered...

In relation to plywood, what does the abbreviation WBP mean?

The abbreviation 'WBP' is used to refer to a type of adhesive; it means 'weather and boil proof', not, as is commonly thought; 'water and boil proof'. The term 'weather' in WBP means that it has a very high resistance to all weather conditions including water, but not just water.

What's the difference between WBP sheathing and shuttering plywood and marine plywood?

Both are bonded using a WBP adhesive: sheathing and shuttering plywood uses lower quality veneers and may contain defects; marine plywood uses premium grade veneers with no gaps or voids in order to withstand complete and prolonged submersion in water.

Select resources for setting out

 ACTIVITY

1. State how a try square can be checked for accuracy.

2. Explain the difference between two sheets of veneered plywood that are listed on a job sheet as 2440 × 1220 mm and 1220 × 2440 mm respectively.

  ACTIVITY

Describe the difference between 'block board' and 'lamin board'.

Setting out for bench joinery and site carpentry

Work procedures

ACTIVITY

Explain what is meant by the following two methods used when specifying purpose-made joinery items and state the implications on the need to take site measurements:

1. Built-in joinery.

2. Fixed-in joinery.

Recognition of joints

ACTIVITY

Look at the illustrations below. Complete the table to name each joint and state a typical use:

Name of joint	Typical use
A	
B	
C	
D	

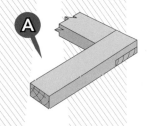
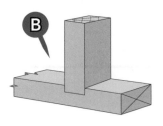
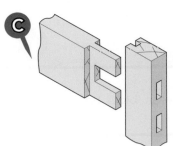
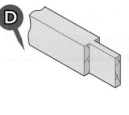
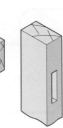

Use of joints

Architects' drawings for items of joinery are often little more than a brief outline, leaving the interpretation of the construction details and jointing to the joinery works.

ACTIVITY

Produce a sketch in the space below to show the joint between the head and jamb of a rebated door casing.

Work procedures

ACTIVITY

Either in a small group or on your own, consider the following real-life problem or scenario:

Peter is one of the newly-qualified bench joiners working for a purpose-made joinery workshop. The company is very busy and Peter has been asked to assist in the setting out section.

Gavin, the head setter-out, has given Peter the drawings and specification for a bookcase that is to be fixed in position once the main building is complete.

Peter considers whether, in view of the short timescales involved, a site visit is required before he starts the setting out.

- Do you think Peter is right to consider this?
- What are the potential implications?
- What is Peter's best course of action?

Set out for bench joinery and site carpentry

ACTIVITY

1. Explain the relationship between the width and thickness of tenons.

2. Other than the actual height and width section, state THREE other pieces of information that should be included on a rod:

   a.

   b.

   c.

3. List the THREE critical sizes used when setting out:

   a.

   b.

   c.

4. Explain in sequence the correct procedure for setting out a workshop rod and name the items of equipment used at each stage.

Setting out crossword

ACTIVITY

Solve the following clues and complete the crossword.

Down

1. Shape and size of joinery in relation to body characteristics.
    _ _ _ _ _ _ _ _ _ _ _ _ _ _ _ (15)

2. Full-size drawing produced by setter out.
    _ _ _ _ _ _ _ _ / _ _ _ (8&3)

3. Decorative profile applied to a timber section.
    _ _ _ _ _ (5)

5. Intermediate vertical member of a window frame. _ _ _ _ _ _ _ (7)

6. Tool used to mark parallel lines n a rod.
    _ _ _ _ _ / _ _ _ _ (5&4)

Across

2. Not the height section. _ _ _ _ _ (5)

4. Not a pictorial method of drawing projection.
    _ _ _ _ _ _ _ _ _ _ _ _ (12)

7. Housing to receive a haunch.
    _ _ _ _ _ _ _ _ _ (9)

8. Refers to general direction of cells in timber.
    _ _ _ _ _ (5)

9. Tool used to mark or test a right angle.
    _ _ _ / _ _ _ _ _ _ (3&6)

QUICK QUIZ

How much do you know about setting out for routine joinery?

1. What scale should be used when setting out workshop rods for joinery items?
   a. 1:1
   b. 1:2
   c. 1:5
   d. 1:10

2. The measurements for joinery items that are specified as 'fixed in' are most accurately obtained:
   a. by measuring on-site
   b. by scaling from the drawing
   c. using those stated in a specification
   d. using those indicated in a plan

3. Ash is a:
   a. white to light brown softwood
   b. white to light brown hardwood
   c. reddish brown softwood
   d. reddish brown hardwood

4. Softwood timbers are:
   a. heavier than hardwoods
   b. softer than hardwoods
   c. cone bearing
   d. broad leaved

5. Which one of the following timbers is the most naturally durable?
   a. redwood
   b. spruce
   c. oak
   d. beech

6. Which one of the following timber-based boards is manufactured using small compressed wood chips or flakes?
   a. fibre board
   b. particle board
   c. block board
   d. strand board

7. The joint normally used between the bottom rail and stile of a panel door is a:
   a. single haunched mortise and tenon
   b. double haunched mortise and tenon
   c. twin haunched mortise and tenon
   d. barefaced mortise and tenon

8. TWO of the following statements are true and TWO are false:
   A rods normally show full-size horizontal and vertical sections
   B a thumb rule is used to draw parallel lines
   C horizontal sections on a rod are normally drawn towards the setter-out
   D the head of vertical sections are normally positioned on the right-hand side
   Which are the true statements?
   a. A and C
   b. C and D
   c. D and B
   d. B and A

9. Anti-capillary grooves are incorporated in window frame sections in order to:
   a. form a moulding around the section
   b. form a rebate to receive the opening casement
   c. prevent the passage of rainwater
   d. restrict the amount of drafts

10. The legal requirements concerning the pitch of a stair, minimum headroom or gaps in a balustrade can be found by reference to:
   a. building regulations
   b. contract documents
   c. CDM regulations
   d. manufacturer's brochure

UNIT 2035

Mark out from setting-out details for routine joinery products

Marking out involves referring to design drawings, workshop rods and cutting lists produced during the setting-out process and the selection and marking out of timbers to show the exact position of joints, mouldings, sections and shapes. In addition, marking out may also include the making of jigs for later manufacturing or assembly operations.

After the timber has been prepared and faces marked, the actual marking out of the item can be undertaken. Depending on the size of the joinery works and the volume of work it handles, setting out and marking out may either be undertaken by one person or treated as separate roles to be undertaken by different people.

Key knowledge:
➤ producing marking out efficiently
➤ producing accurate marking out.

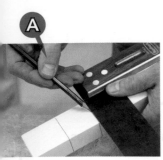

Producing accurate marking out

Marking out tools and equipment

ACTIVITY

Look at the photographs in the margin. Name each tool or piece of equipment and state what it is used for:

A

B

C

Using patterns

The first components marked out become the patterns for the rest of the job. After checking for accuracy, they can be used for marking out other pieces and setting up machines.

ACTIVITY

Look at the illustration below, which shows a marked-out pattern jamb of a door frame, then complete the following:

1. Produce a sketch to show a typical pattern for the head of the same frame.

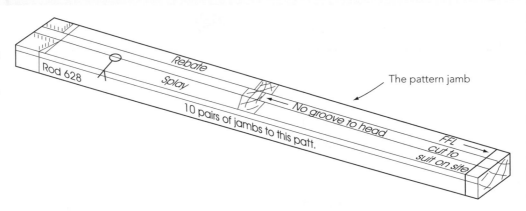

Rod 628

Rebate

Splay

The pattern jamb

No groove to head

10 pairs of jambs to this patt.

FFL
cut to
suit on site

2. What does the abbreviation 'FFL' on the pattern mean?

Accurate marking out

ACTIVITY

1. Describe how the details contained on a workshop rod are transferred to the timber sections.

2. State the reason why a batch of paired stiles may be cramped to a pattern for marking out.

3. Explain what happens to the pattern components produced during marking out.

key terms

Storey rod: a timber batten marked with the total vertical rise of a staircase from the finished floor level at the bottom to the finished floor level at the top.

Going rod: a timber batten marked with the total horizontal distance of travel from the nosing of the bottom step to the nosing of the upper floor or landing.

Setting-out rod: full-size vertical and horizontal section of an item showing the position and profile of components and the method of jointing.

Avoiding marking out confusion

ACTIVITY

Either in a small group or on your own, consider the following real-life scenario:

Rob is one of the apprentice bench joiners working for a purpose-made joinery workshop. As part of his training, he has been asked to assist in marking out flights of stairs for a local housing refurbishment contract.

Davila, a newly-qualified bench joiner, visited each house and made a **storey rod** and a **going rod** for each. On returning to the workshop, these were used to prepare **setting-out rods**, to which she taped the relevant storey and going rod before passing on to Rob for marking out.

On checking the storey and going rod and setting-out rod for the first flight, Rob noticed that the storey rod measured 2580 mm but the setting-out rod stated that the stair had 12 steps, each with a rise of 214.5 mm. However, on checking further, the storey rod did seem to match the setting out for another house.

- What has gone wrong?

- What should Davila do to resolve the situation?

- What should be done in future to prevent a recurrence of the situation?

Marking out: true or false

 ACTIVITY

Read the following statements and place a tick in the appropriate boxes:

Statement	True	False
Anthropometrics is the name given to the size and shape of joinery.		
A box square is used to protect try squares.		
A 'weathered' joinery section has a sloping surface.		
Workshop rods drawn on paper are considered to be more dimensionally stable than those drawn on plywood.		
Patterns are used when setting out repetitive items of joinery.		
It is standard practice to draw the width rod before the height rod.		
Tangential sawn timber sections are preferred for joinery as they are less likely to distort after conversion.		
Book matching refers to the selection of veneers from a supplier's catalogue.		
Marking out of the rod is done before the setting out of the joinery components.		
The head of a joinery frame is normally drawn on a rod to the left.		
Mitres are always cut at a 45° angle.		
Setting out is the process of marking the actual joints and sections, etc. on the timber components.		
FAS is an abbreviation related to the grading of hardwoods.		
The sight size and shoulder size of a door rail are the same.		
Twin tenons are formed in the width of a section one above the other, whereas double tenons are formed in the thickness of a section side by side.		
The abbreviation MDF refers to the type of adhesive used to manufacture timber-based sheet material.		
The width of a mortise is normally governed by the size of chisel available.		
Aesthetics is the term used when relating the size of the human body to joinery items.		

Marking out wordsearch

 ACTIVITY

Hidden in the word square are the following 20 words associated with marking out. You may find the words written forwards, backwards, up, down or diagonally.

Draw a ring around the words, or a line through them using a highlighter pen.

You will need to become familiar with these terms. Look up any that you are unsure of in a textbook or undertake a web search.

Marking out	Inaccuracies	Mortise
Batch	Rebate	CAD/CAM
Patter	Prepared	Box square
Sectional	Rectangular	Shoulder lines
Going	Chamfer	Paired
Accuracy	Handed	Straight edge
Squared	Face side	

B	P	C	N	E	S	M	F	H	N	R	C	U	E	I
I	A	P	O	Y	C	A	D	C	A	M	U	B	E	R
P	I	T	E	G	C	N	P	L	R	G	M	I	D	S
X	R	O	C	E	R	A	U	Q	S	X	O	B	D	U
U	E	E	S	H	T	G	R	T	E	S	R	I	C	B
P	D	I	P	T	N	A	M	U	I	C	E	D	N	A
E	D	I	E	A	C	O	B	I	C	H	F	G	R	G
E	I	R	T	N	R	T	O	E	A	C	M	C	H	E
A	L	C	R	T	R	E	G	N	R	R	A	I	D	T
S	E	N	I	L	R	E	D	L	U	O	H	S	E	U
R	E	S	G	G	T	E	D	L	C	A	C	R	R	C
Y	E	R	D	U	D	R	E	Y	C	I	I	R	A	T
U	T	U	O	G	N	I	K	R	A	M	D	G	U	E
T	A	S	S	E	C	T	I	O	N	A	L	N	Q	C
L	A	E	G	D	E	T	H	G	I	A	R	T	S	E

QUICK QUIZ How much do you know about marking out for routine joinery?

1. The purpose of a workshop briefing between the setter/marker-out, joiners and machinists prior to the making of a prototype for a new item of joinery is to:
   a. discuss health and safety issues
   b. ensure the item is completed on time
   c. discuss specific technical issues
   d. motivate all concerned

2. Which one of the following squares is best used to mark around pre-moulded timber sections.
   a. try square
   b. set square
   c. box square
   d. combination square

3. What is the main purpose of using a setting-out rod when marking out joinery?
   a. ensure the correct number of items
   b. enable the selection of tools and equipment
   c. help to maintain a consistent finish
   d. maintain accurate positioning of members and overall sizes

4. In relation to the person marking out sections from a rod, the correct positioning of face and edge marks on a section are:
   a. face up, edge furthest away from person
   b. face up, edge closest to person
   c. face down, edge furthest away from person
   d. face down, edge closest to person

5. Which one of the following statements is correct?
   a. all sections showing defects or distortion should be discarded
   b. minor defects can be positioned so that they will be unseen in the finished work
   c. grain direction or slope is not relevant to the marker out
   d. panels should have any arched top grain features pointing downwards

6. Which one of the following operations is not regarded as marking out?
   a. making of patterns and jigs
   b. drawing of height and width sections
   c. selection of timbers and sheet material
   d. establishing the position of joints

7. The first course of action to take when an error is found in the information being used for marking out would be to:
   a. speak to your supervisor, before proceeding any further
   b. try to find out what was done in the past, and make the choice yourself
   c. speak to your supervisor at the end of the day to obtain the correct information
   d. ignore it if it's not your mistake and allow an extra tolerance so that it will fit

8. When marking out a large batch of door stiles:
   a. a rod is not required as the marking out can be done from the pattern
   b. each stile should be fully marked out individually from the rod
   c. one stile should be fully marked out and used as a pattern for the others
   d. it is best to mark out the pattern first, which can then be used to draw the rod

9. The finished size of a section is:
   a. the dimension after planing
   b. the dimension before planing
   c. the dimension before sawing
   d. the dimension after sawing

10. Which of the following is the odd one out?
    a. stile
    b. rail
    c. muntin
    d. jamb

UNIT 2036

Manufacture routine joinery products

Joiners undertaking the manufacture of routine joinery products will be involved in the fitting, assembling and finishing of pre-machined components to form a range of joinery products including:

➤ doors
➤ windows
➤ door frames and linings
➤ staircases
➤ units and fitments.

Key knowledge:
➤ selecting the correct materials
➤ manufacturing joinery.

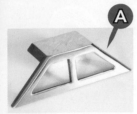
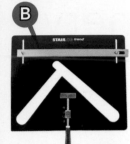

Selecting the correct materials

Tools and equipment

ACTIVITY

Look at the photographs. Name the tool or piece of equipment and state what each is used for:

A

B

C

ACTIVITY

In the space below, compile a list of tools and equipment that you would require in order to assemble a traditional casement sash:

Your questions answered...

What is 'winding' in an item of framed joinery and how can it be avoided?

A joinery item is said to be winding or in-wind if it is distorted or not flat. Winding can be avoided by checking the framed joinery item with winding strips at the dry assembly and final assembly stages to ensure it is flat or out-of-wind.

Manufacturing joinery

ACTIVITY

Look at the illustration of a traditional half-glazed panel door and answer the following:

1. Name the joint used where the glazing bars intersect.

2. State the reason for using a diminished stile.

3. State the commonly used name for the diminished stile.

4. What is a bolection mould?

5. The glazing bars are sub-tenoned into the stiles. Explain how they can be secured with wedges.

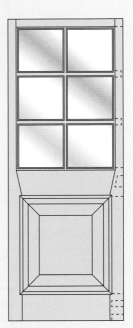

ACTIVITY

The following component parts and terms are associated with joinery items:

Stile	Jamb	String	Nosing	Muntin
Transom	Mullion	Haunched	Barefaced	Drawbored
Rail	Standard	Potboard	Weathered	

Using a computer, place the terms in a table, state what they mean and give an example of where they might be used.

Manufacturing joinery

ACTIVITY

1. Explain the difference in methods used to prepare planed joinery items to receive either a clear lacquer or painted finish.

2. State what a mitre template or box mitre is used for.

3. A door is specified in a schedule using the abbreviation FD30S. Explain what this means.

ACTIVITY

In the space below, produce sketches and brief notes to explain the difference between 'out-of-wind' and 'in-wind' or 'winding' when checking the flatness of a framed joinery item during assembly.

What is a blind mortise and tenon joint?

A blind mortise and tenon joint is where the mortise slot is stopped short and does not pass completely through the timber section. It is also known as a stopped mortise and tenon joint.

Manufacturing joinery wordsearch

ACTIVITY

Hidden in the word square are the following 20 words associated with manufacturing joinery. You may find the words written forwards, backwards, up, down or diagonally.

Draw a ring around the words, or a line through them using a highlighter pen.

You will need to become familiar with these terms. Look up any that you are unsure of in a textbook or undertake a web search.

Joinery	Light	Casement	Barefaced
Sash	Rod	Traditional	Workshop
Matchboard	Cutting list	Stormproof	Window
Stile	Door	Rail	Squaring
Mullion	Winding	Jamb	Allowance

Y	R	E	N	I	O	J	E	L	R	E	S	J
O	E	C	D	N	T	L	D	Y	I	Q	W	R
U	S	N	U	R	I	A	O	L	U	A	O	O
B	M	A	J	T	A	N	O	A	A	W	R	O
N	E	W	S	C	T	O	R	K	O	L	K	N
T	C	O	P	H	Q	I	B	D	L	I	S	O
N	I	L	A	L	N	T	N	H	C	G	H	I
E	W	L	E	G	S	I	J	G	C	H	O	L
M	Q	A	H	A	W	D	Q	T	L	T	P	L
E	B	A	R	E	F	A	C	E	D	I	A	U
S	T	O	R	M	P	R	O	O	F	W	S	M
A	D	R	H	O	A	T	E	G	D	T	M	T
C	W	I	N	D	I	N	G	C	T	R	L	Q

QUICK QUIZ — How much do you know about manufacturing routine joinery products?

1. What is the best way of checking an assembled frame for square?
   a. using the 3:4:5 rule
   b. using winding strips
   c. measuring the two diagonals
   d. checking each corner with a try square

2. The component that is used to finish the top step of a flight of timber stairs is termed a:
   a. lining
   b. capping
   c. string
   d. nosing

3. How many goings will there be in a flight of stairs that has 14 risers?
   a. 12
   b. 13
   c. 14
   d. 15

4. A plastic laminate is to be bonded to an MDF work surface using a contact adhesive. The two surfaces can be brought into contact:
   a. after five minutes
   b. when the adhesive is touch dry
   c. directly after the adhesive has been applied
   d. when the spirit smell is no longer given off

5. The going of a step is measured from the:
   a. face of one riser to the face of the next riser
   b. edge of the nosing to the face of riser
   c. face of one riser to the back of the next riser
   d. face of one tread to the face of the next tread

6. Which one of the following adhesives has to be mixed with water before use?
   a. PVA
   b. polyurethane
   c. casein
   d. epoxy resin

7. The term 'door set' refers to:
   a. a door that has been pre-hung in a frame or lining before installation
   b. a twisted or distorted door that does not close into its frame properly
   c. the hinges, lock or latch and associated furniture fitted to a door
   d. a matched pair of doors, often termed as a French window

8. Why should panels in framed joinery be assembled dry and not glued to the framing members?
   a. gluing makes it more difficult to assemble
   b. the glue can spoil the panel finish
   c. the frame should be strong enough without gluing the panels
   d. to allow movement between the panel and the framework

9. The term 'spandrel' is associated with stairs. It refers to the:
   a. triangular block that reinforces the joint between tread and riser
   b. triangular-shaped treads used to turn a flight around a corner
   c. structure that provides support to the centre of wide flights
   d. triangular-shaped area between the outer string and the floor

10. Which one of the following statements concerning adhesives is true?
   a. PVA adhesive can be used for bonding plastic laminates without the use of a mechanical press
   b. casein is a powdered adhesive made from soured milk curds, which is mixed with water before use
   c. formaldehyde-based adhesives are only suitable for the general assembly of internal joinery
   d. the 'pot life' of an adhesive refers to the amount of time the unmixed components can be stored before they start to deteriorate